# BEHIND BARS

# BEHIND BARS

*Inside Ontario's Heritage Gaols*

## RON BROWN

NATURAL HERITAGE BOOKS
TORONTO

Published by Natural Heritage / Natural History Inc.
PO Box 95, Station O, Toronto, Ontario  M4A 2M8
www.naturalheritagebooks.com

All visuals courtesy of the author, unless otherwise credited.
*Front cover, from top left*: carving of felon's head (Woodstock jail);
"Coby" jail in Coboconk; Warden's house, Kingston Penitentiary;
Waterloo County jail in Kitchener; cells in Carleton County jail (Ottawa);
the restored lock-up in Beaverton; Governor's house in Cayuga.
*Back cover, top*, part of the original yard wall at the Wellington County jail (Guelph); *bottom left*, the jail at L'Orignal; *bottom right*, a former jail cell converted into a guest room in Cobourg.

Cover design by Neil Thorne
Book design by Norton Hamill Design
Edited by Jane Gibson

Printed and bound in Canada by Hignell Book Printing

*Library and Archives Canada Cataloguing in Publication*
Brown, Ron, 1945-
Behind bars : inside Ontario's heritage gaols / Ron Brown.
Includes bibliographical references and index.
ISBN 1-897045-17-4
1. Jails—Ontario—History. 2. Ontario—History, Local. I. Title.
HV8746.C32B76 2006      365'.9713      C2006-904171-7

Natural Heritage / Natural History Inc. acknowledges the financial support of the Canada Council for the Arts and the Ontario Arts Council for our publishing program. We acknowledge the support of the Government of Ontario through the Ontario Media Development Corporation's Ontario Book Initiative. We also acknowledge the financial support of the Government of Canada through the Book Publishing Industry Development Program (BPIDP) and the Association for the Export of Canadian Books.

*I want to dedicate this book to my family for enduring my absences while researching Ontario's heritage jails, although they may have, on occasion, wished that my time "behind bars" was a little longer. Nor should we forget those who have, for various reasons, spent time unjustly in the dark confines of our jails.*

# Contents

# Acknowledgements

I am happy to give considerable credit to those who tend what I consider the researcher's most useful source of information, the local library. Here are files filled with anecdotes, newspaper clippings and unpublished accounts, which contain many of the more colourful stories about their community's local history. I wish to thank the curators of the museums in Gore Bay, Beaverton, Napanee, Tweed and Cayuga for their particular help, as well municipal staff in Brockville, Cornwall, L'Orignal and Guelph, and a thank you to Chris Raible of Creemore for background on the "Windsor Raids" of 1838. My gratitude goes, too, to the cops, the cons and the retired corrections officers who provided me with their candid insights into Ontario's heritage "gaols." Lastly, I want to thank my daughter, Jeri, for her valuable work as my research assistant for this project.

# Introduction

Go to a jail in Ontario today, and you are likely to leave as easily as you entered, voluntarily and with a smile. The reason is simple—most of the early lock-ups in this province are no longer used for incarceration. Rather, where there were cells that once held hardened thieves, hookers, or just the itinerant or the insane, there are now books, or filing cabinets, or desks, or...cells.

While most have been renovated into town halls, law offices, libraries or government departments, leaving the facades alone as the sole legacy of their distinctive heritage, others, such as those at Goderich and Gore Bay are preserved entirely as jail museums, while those at London, Brampton, Ottawa and Cobourg, have retained portions of their old jail features. The little lock-ups at Beaverton, Creemore, Manitowaning and Woodslee have also been preserved as jailhouse museums, while at Coboconk and Port Dalhousie, a gift shop and bar, respectively, now occupy the cell areas. Sadly, recent and ill-considered demolitions of the county jails in St. Thomas, Kingston, Hamilton, and especially that in St. Catharines, have robbed modern-day residents in those communities of a part of their legacy, even though it may be a dark legacy and one that some would just as soon overlook.

The reader may wonder what criteria the author has chosen to define a "heritage" jail. Quite simply, a "heritage" jail for this book is one that was built prior to the era of the Ontario Provincial Police (OPP), and one that is visually distinct from related buildings such as town halls and courthouses. With the inauguration of the new province-wide police force on October 13, 1909, modern lock-ups began to be included as detention cells within police stations. These

represent an era of centralization, modernization and the needs of the
auto age, while the dismal dungeons of the past reflect an Ontario
whose like will never be seen again.

As with most of the books that this author has written, the aim is to
encourage readers to explore and celebrate the legacy of a bygone era
in Ontario. But unlike the criminal, the vagrant, or the insane, who
once lurked within those dank confines of Ontario's heritage "gaols,"
readers can leave as easily as they enter.

# BEHIND BARS

# 1

# GOING TO GAOL

"The prison [at Alba Fucens in central Italy] is a deep underground dungeon, dark and noisesome…with so many shut up in such close quarters, the poor wretches were reduced to the appearance of brutes. And since the food and everything pertaining to their other needs were so foully commingled, a stench so terrible assailed anyone who drew near it that it could scarcely be endured." Such is the disturbing scene depicted by the 1st century AD scribe named Diodorus Siculus.[1]

Another early depiction of ancient prisons comes from historian Sallust who described the 2nd century AD prison in the Roman forum as "a place about 12 feet below the surface of the ground. It is enclosed on all side by walls…Neglect, darkness and stench make it hideous, and fearsome to behold."[2] The need to restrain misfits, and to punish evil-doers is as old as human society itself. With the evolution of cities and the political institutions to govern them, rules were written and dungeons constructed to formalize the reasons and the places for such incarcerations.

In England, the evolution of the jail system began following the conquest of England in 1066 by William of Normandy, who built the first Tower of London. A century later, Henry II ordered his sheriffs to build jails in each county. During this period, however, except for the notorious Tower, prisons were used to house misfits and not to punish crimes. Actual punishment usually consisted of mutilation, humiliation, exile or execution. Many an early prison became infamous over the centuries. Besides the Tower of London, a popular London attraction to this day, there was the Doge's prison in Venice. Although one

The famous Tower of London is now a popular tourist attraction in England.

of the city's most beautiful buildings on the outside, it was a brutish dungeon on the inside where anyone could end up based solely on an anonymous letter; no proof needed.

In France, the Bastille is renowned for its role in the start of the French Revolution when the citizens stormed it to free political prisoners. Devil's Island was a feared penal colony, which the French operated in the steamy south Caribbean from 1887 until 1938, and was the locale for the popular movie, "Papillon."

The first effort at incarceration for the purpose of reforming the inmate was that at Bridewell Palace in London, and was used largely to reform vagrants. In 1609, King James I required each county to open a "bridewell" as they came to be called. With the arrival of the Industrial Revolution in the late 18th century, prisons were used to reform the "misguided" lower classes, and make them into better workers. Indeed, it was common practice for prisoners to be "rented" to factory owners as a source of cheap labour.

Prior to the wide-scale settlement of Upper Canada (later Ontario), lock-ups were confined to military garrisons, although a publicly subscribed jail may have been built in Gananoque during this time.[3] When Upper Canada was created under British law, following the arrival of the United Empire Loyalists,[4] the notion of the jail was to detain an accused until the appropriate punishment could be meted out.

Over the decades, three levels of "gaol" appeared in Ontario—the county jail, the local lock-up, and the federal penitentiary, or "big house." To administer the colony, Upper Canada's first administrator, Lieutenant-Governor John Graves Simcoe, divided the area into four districts, and in each district appointed justices of the peace to carry out the law, complete with a courthouse and jail. At first these were little more than two-storey log buildings with the court above and the cells below. They were located at New Johnstown (Cornwall) for the Eastern District, Kingston for the Midland District, Newark (Niagara-on-the-Lake) for the Home District, and L'Assomption (Sandwich, later Windsor) for the Western District.

But even from the start, the jails were notoriously inadequate. With little funding to provide security, escapes were routine and jailers were, on occasion, required to keep prisoners locked in their own homes. The scarcity of funds also forced the legislature to require that two cells in each jail be set aside as "bridewells" and so began the tradition of Ontario's jails housing the poor and the insane together with the criminals. In fact, in many cases, inspection reports showed the jails as containing more "non-criminals" than criminals.

By 1826 the four original districts had been further divided into eleven, and, by the 1840s, district jails had been completed in Cornwall, Kingston, Niagara, York, Sandwich (Windsor), Brockville, Cobourg, London, L'Orignal, Hamilton, Perth, Picton, Barrie, Simcoe, Woodstock, Goderich, Peterborough, Belleville, Ottawa and Guelph. Following the creation of the county system of government in 1849, Ontario grew into an administrative system of 42 counties,[5] with Dufferin County the last to be formed in 1881.

As with the districts, to qualify for separate municipal status, each county was required to erect a courthouse and jail. In many cases the jails were simply a wing added to the rear of the courthouse. In other cases, the jails were constructed separate from the courthouse, many displaying the finest architectural styles of the day, from Romanesque, to Italianate, to Classical, or to Gothic.

Meanwhile, newly created municipalities, such as towns, townships, villages and cities, were empowered to create their own constabularies and to construct lock-ups. Established places like York and Hamilton already had their own courts and jails as early as the mid-1830s. In the new municipalities, cells were usually situated in the basements of the

Entombment in this coffin-like box was a common form of punishment. This device is on display at the Prison Museum in Kingston.

town halls. In other cases, as well as in "police" villages,[6] separate lock-ups might be constructed. These small jails ranged from a single cell up to as many as five. They were the responsibility of a local constable whose myriad other responsibilities might have ranged from rounding up stray animals to sweeping the streets. With the creation of the Ontario Provincial Police in 1909,[7] many of these jails were replaced by detention cells in newly built OPP stations.

The third level of prison was the "penitentiary." It was here that prisoners were sent as "penance," to serve out long sentences. While the local lock-ups or county jails were intended only for short-term stays, the penitentiary replaced the gallows for many of the hundreds of petty crimes for which the penalty was death. Ontario's first "pen" was one at Portsmouth near Kingston, which opened in 1835. It was followed by the Central Prison in Toronto, built in 1875, and other federal penitentiaries at Collins Bay, Millhaven, Joyceville, and a new women's pen,[8] all in the Kingston area.

In northern Ontario, where districts still existed, the Ontario Department of Public Works undertook the building of the courthouses and jails, and, from the 1870s, appointed provincial constables to police them. By 1897 in addition to the district jails, a dozen local lock-ups had been built across the north by the Ontario government.

But local autonomy was not serving the jails well. By the late 1850s local politicians, after having been obliged to build the jails, showed little interest in maintaining them. In 1860, the Board of Inspectors for provincial gaols and asylums issued a memo on the "Construction and Management of Common Gaols." The jails, they observed, were "in their present state an obstacle to discipline and reform."[9] Among the reforms proposed, the memo included the separation of prisoners on the basis of sex, age, moral character and degree of guilt. Physically, the facilities should include hardwood floors, wrought iron doors, outside privies and ventilation to the outside. Cell ranges should be internal and constructed back to back. To make sure that these regulations were followed, a system of regular inspections was established. To this day, the reports of the "common gaol" inspectors provide some of the most vivid accounts of the grim life inside Ontario's early jails.

This directive was replaced in 1881 by a still more detailed order-in-council which listed 100 regulations for the "Government of Common Gaols of Ontario."[10] These included job descriptions for the sheriff who oversaw the jails of the county, for the "gaoler" who was responsible for their day-to-day operation, and for the "turnkey" who watched the inmates directly, as well as regulations governing matrons and jail surgeons.

The list prescribed prisoners' activities, clothes and meals. Punishments included the "hard bed," a diet of bread and water, or confinement in a dark cell, and could be imposed for such infractions as assault, indecent behaviour, bad language, or simply for neglecting to keep the cell clean. Punishments in the penitentiaries were considerably more brutal, and included floggings, water torture and entombment.

As for the jail buildings themselves, the order decreed that no animals shall be kept in the yards, that no wood or other material shall be piled against the walls, that no trees or shrubs shall be planted in the jail yard, that no privies shall be located

This punishment mechanism, a type of water torture, is on display at the Kingston Prison Museum. It gave prisoners the sensation of being drowned.

inside the buildings, and that padlocks shall weigh no less than two-and-a-half pounds. The final regulation of that directive resonates to this day with journalists as "no person shall be allowed access to any prisoner for the purpose of interviewing him or her, with a view to publishing a report of such interview."[11]

Despite these requirements, criticism continued to be heaped upon Ontario's jails even up until recent times with modern-day grand juries calling them "black holes" and "unfit" for humans. Finally, in 1968, the province took over administration of the county jails and within less than a decade had closed 19 of the worst.[12] With the introduction of the super-jail concept in the later 1990s, many of the remaining "county" jails were closed as well.

Within those walls, the ghosts of the many who were executed may still be watching. Prior to 1760, more than 150 offences were punishable by death. By the time Upper Canada's first jails were under construction, this had been reduced to 12. By 1841 the number had been dropped to three—murder, rape and treason. From Confederation until the abolition of capital punishment in 1976, Canada employed its own official executioner. Not surprisingly, to avoid retribution by families of those executed, few of Canada's hangmen used their own names. In fact, one name, Ellis, was the pseudonym most commonly used during that time.

The name originated with Arthur English, cousin of England's hangman who had adopted the phony name of "John Ellis." English was hired in 1913 and adopted the name Arthur Ellis. After presiding over 600 executions around the world, he quit when he miscalculated the weight of a woman who had been sentenced to death, resulting in her torso severing from her head. Following his retirement in 1938, he was replaced by another "Arthur Ellis." Canada's last hangman used "John Ellis" and continued in this capacity for several years following the formal abolition of capital punishment in Canada. (Some capital offences remained under the National Defence Act for a few more years.)

Canada's last hanging occurred in 1962 with the double execution of Arthur Lucas and Ronald Turpin in Toronto's Don Jail. Lucas had murdered Thomas Crater and Carol Newman, while Turpin had murdered police constable Fred Nash. Years later, the judge who had sentenced Turpin to his fate reflected that the one good thing about Turpin's execution was that it was Canada's last.

# 2

# THE COUNTY GAOLS

**A**s the 18th century drew to a close, what we call Ontario today was an untamed wilderness. Aside from the small groups of Aboriginal peoples, its few permanent inhabitants were French settlers along the Detroit River, and military settlements near Kingston, York and Newark (Niagara-on-the-Lake). With the end of the American Revolution, refugees who had remained loyal to England streamed northward to avoid persecution and death in the former American colonies. At that time, the only incarceration facilities were to be found in military garrisons.

As more and more settlers arrived, Upper Canada was divided into four districts. To accommodate the spreading settlement, these districts were further subdivided until finally in 1849, the area became a system of counties whose governing councils were responsible for roads, land registry and courts. In fact, no county would be approved without the building of a courthouse and jail. Towns that were selected as county towns grew quickly and many would soon boast beautifully designed courthouses.

## BARRIE

For those who love their heritage buildings, Barrie is a less than ideal destination. Over the years most of its key structures have been removed—the downtown railway station, the city hall, the post office, the courthouse and many less significant buildings as well. Now that the ancient jail has been closed, one can only hope that the same fate will not befall it as well.

The historic Simcoe County jail in Barrie is now closed.

Historians write that the jail is the only building left in the city that ties it directly to the creation of the District of Simcoe. In 1837, Simcoe was separated from the earlier "Home District" and Barrie was chosen as the district seat. In 1841, the required courthouse and jail were finished. They were located on what is today Mulcaster Street, originally named Market Street. Designed by Thomas Young,[1] the jail was built to resemble that in Goderich, with an octagonal centre section, and was described at the time as "something like the Mosque of Omar on the site of the Temple of Jerusalem."[2]

Prisoners entered through a long hallway that had walls that narrowed as the prisoner went further inside. This passageway led to a second door and the central section. In 1863, the jail was enlarged and the original third storey tower removed to be replaced with a cupola, which contained a lantern designed to illuminate the radiating corridors. The stone for the building was extracted from a quarry at Longford on the east side of Lake Couchiching.

Despite the security breakouts did occur. In 1876, two prisoners, while in the "airing" yard, broke the padlock to another yard where they wrenched the door from the privy, and, lodging it against another door, vaulted over the wall. That was not a good year for the Barrie jail as the prison inspector also complained that the "gaol was in a most disorderly state, with the lowest kind of discipline. The beds were filthy and the walls begrimed with smoke...the turnkey has been absent for a week, leaving the gaoler in charge who let [the prisoners] do as they wished."[3] He also found a woman incarcerated with her two sons for "no crime other than being homeless (and) forced to live with criminals." He urged, in vain, the construction of a county poor house.

One of the most publicized crimes at the county jail was that of the murder of John Strathy, a local bank manager. On February 19, 1896, one Michael Brennan, who was estranged from his wife and children, entered Strathy's home. He demanded that Strathy tell him where his children were. When Strathy confronted him, Brennan shot him through the heart. While Strathy lay dying, Brennan coolly left the house and hitched a ride into town where he surrendered to Sheriff Drury.

A close-up of the entrance to the Barrie jail provides details of the stone work.

During the trial, Brennan's wife tried to convince the jury that her husband was insane. Disregarding her pleas, the jury found him guilty and sentenced him to hang. The jury at a second trial, on appeal, also convicted him but recommended mercy. Six days before he was to be hanged, his sentence was commuted to life in prison. The jail, however, did witness five hangings, including that of Lloyd Simcoe in 1945; he was 18 years old, convicted of murder.

The exterior of the jail has changed little over the years, although much of the interior has been modernized. In 1877, the original courthouse, a mundane piece of architecture, was totally altered, and then, in 1977, was demolished to make way for a new county building. The jail was closed in January of 2002. The building sits on a hill at the southeast corner of Mulcaster and MacDonald streets in Barrie, several blocks north of the downtown area.

## BRAMPTON

The Brampton jail in the Peel Heritage Complex remains one of Ontario's most easily visited lock-ups, as one of Ontario's most famous inmates would earlier discover.

The Peel County jail in Brampton once hosted American fugitive Huey Newton.

Since its completion in 1867, the Brampton jail has housed thousands of prisoners, with three being executed. But perhaps its most celebrated guest arrived in 1977, the much publicized American "Black Panther," Huey Newton. Having previously fled from Cuba, where he had been living as a fugitive from the United States, Newton wanted to consult with lawyers in Canada before surrendering to U.S. authorities. He was escorted to the Brampton jail while those consultations took place. With its ancient cells measuring a mere one by two metres, the jail was, complained Newton, "worse than any jail in Cuba."[4] That view, it seems, was shared by more than just the jail's inmates. In 1968, a grand jury labelled it an "ugly pile of stone…It is hard to express the utter distaste this monstrous anachronism arouses."[5]

It took nine more years before the inadequate jail was finally closed, and another eight before it became one of Ontario's better jail museums. Along with the courthouse and registry office, the jail had been built to satisfy the requirements of Peel County's newly acquired status as a separate county jurisdiction.

Like most early jails, the one in Brampton endured its share of escapes. In 1888, a murderer by the name of Preston fled by simply placing a bench on a table and scrambling up on it and from there over the high wall. He was last seen in nearby Huttonville. Two more inmates escaped at meal time in 1906 by going through a door that was not locked securely. Once outside they wrenched a pump from the ground and used it to scale the wall.

Others, on the other hand, did not leave at all. During its existence, the Brampton jail witnessed three executions. In 1909, Stefan Swyryda was hanged for the murder of a fellow Polish immigrant—the 17-year-old Olack Leutick. In 1941, Gordon Mathews died for the murder of his wife, while in 1946, Walter Zabolotny was executed for murdering Alice Campbell during a robbery attempt. This would be the jail's final death sentence. For the most part, however, inmates consisted of drunks, vagrants and those awaiting a court appearance.

In 1882, a vagrant died after a long drive to the jail in poor weather. A grand jury concluded that he should have been taken to the hospital for treatment and that he died as a result of inhumane treatment. The Great Depression of the '30s brought with it transients in search of not just jobs but a hot meal and a bed as well, and the local jail was a common port of call. But at times the cells were too full, and many were forced to sleep on the jail's doorstep after being turned away.

Seven boys, aged 13 to 17, appeared before a judge in Brampton in 1932. They were facing multiple charges of breaking and entering. The judge gave them the option of jail or the strap. After the boys elected jail, the judge was sufficiently impressed by their repentant attitude that he let them off with a suspended entrance.

Now a museum, the jail is a three-storey stone structure, that faces the street independently of the courthouse, making it one of Ontario's most visible heritage jails. While a new wing has now been added to the west side and the upper floors have been totally renovated to accommodate museum displays and meeting rooms, the aura of the jail survives on the ground level. Here are examples of the tiny cells that enclosed the inmates, where one would remain while contemplating "his" fate. The prison doctor's office has also been put on display, and around the wall are accounts of life in the county jail. The front portion of the jail housed the governor and his family until 1961. The exercise or "airing" yard wall now surrounds a parking lot, a place where prisoners would once have spent their outside time in smashing rocks to be used for the building of roads or for construction in general.

With its easy access and frequent hours, Brampton's Heritage Complex. located on the south side of Wellington Street east of Main Street, is a heritage jail, well worth a visit. Even Huey Newton might agree. But then again maybe not.

## BRANTFORD

The jail in Brantford, along with the courthouse, was built in 1852, as a condition of Brant County being granted municipal status. Its original capacity was for twenty men and three women.

The first hanging, a twosome, took place just seven years after the jail was opened. The crime was the murder of a mail carrier named Adams by a trio of thieves identified as Armstrong, Over and Moore. Armstrong was the first to be captured and agreed, in exchange for a life sentence, to implicate his two unfortunate colleagues. Over and Moore were led to the gallows located in a park opposite the jail where a crowd of 8500 had assembled (Brantford's population was only 5000 at the time) to watch them die. Once up on the gallows, they sang a hymn before being plunged to their deaths. Some have suggested that racism may have played a role as Armstrong, who was given the life sentence, was white while the two who died were of African ancestry. To further muddy the waters, the supposed "confessions" of the two unfortunates were "signed" by two men who were so illiterate they didn't know how to write their own names.

Eight more executions were to follow, although after 1868, public hangings had been banned. Ben Carrier of the Six Nations Reserve was hanged for axing his wife to death after she accused him of infidelity. He was followed by Joe Bennett of Oshweken, who raped and strangled one Betsy Jacob; James Taylor who raped and then slit the throat of a 13-year-old boy; George Jones who stabbed his married lover because she had rejected him for her husband; Harry Dent who murdered and dismembered his landlord and Maltese immigrants Caranello and Calleja for killing a fellow immigrant, Gio Batta Bunello. The last execution at Brantford's jail was that of Joseph Barberry who shot his wife in the back after she confronted him over his infidelity and laziness. The hanging took place in 1932.

But the one murder case, which captured the most press, was that of restaurant worker Bob Wong. He had stabbed a fellow restaurant worker over an unpaid mahjong gambling debt. At first the local Chinese community refused to cooperate with the investigation until the possibility of a vicious Tong war[6] raised its head. At that point Wong was pointed out and arrested. The accused, however, could understand neither English nor the legal system. To help him appreciate the

The Brant County jail in Brantford remains in use.

gravity of his testimony, a Chinese translator had Wong swear upon a broken saucer saying, "You shall tell the truth and the whole truth…this saucer is cracked and if you do not tell the truth your soul will be cracked like the saucer."[7] Wong's excuse of self defense was rejected, and he was executed, a steep price to pay for a debt that amounted to $2.50.

Until the 1930s, a bizarre collection of knots from the hangman's ropes remained in the jail, each inscribed with the name of the condemned men, but those have since disappeared. Although the jail was upgraded in 1957 with the addition of a 32-bed wing that included TV and showers, many of the old cells, with their scant 86 centimetres by three metre dimensions (beds in the cells were 76 centimetres by two metres), remained in use. However, the death chamber on the narrow second floor hallway, where the majority of the condemned prisoners awaited their death sentences, was removed. However, the cover above the gallows' trap door can still be seen today. Inside, near the cells, a cramped cell of just one-and-a-half metres square was to used to punish inmates who disturbed other prisoners, or who cursed the guards.

While many of the structures that surround Brantford's historic Victoria Square have been designated as heritage buildings, the jail, which is still in use as of 2006, has remained exempt. The jail itself is located at the rear of the courthouse. The original limestone cell blocks can be seen above the walls built later to surround it. Beside the wall, the governor's dwelling, now containing police offices, still survives as well.

The courthouse, jail and governor's house sit on the east side of Market Street north of Victoria Street near downtown Brantford.

## BROCKVILLE

Compared to the wars with the Americans, it was but a small skirmish, but the battle for the Brockville courthouse and jail was both real and bloody. It all began in 1792 when the town of Johnstown[8] was laid out in the heart of Loyalist country on the shore of the St. Lawrence. By decree of Lieutenant-Governor Simcoe, the fledgling village became the capital of the newly formed Eastern District. Also by decree, each capital was required to have a courthouse and jail. Consequently, a new log jail and courthouse were built in the town site. Annual expenses for the jail, including heating, wages and food amounted to a mere twelve pounds. The log jail offered little in the way of security, however, lacking even a fence around the yard.

In 1808, following a shift in the district boundaries, Johnstown no longer found itself in the centre of the district, and the district seat was moved to a mill site further west called Elizabethtown. The residents of the Johnstown area, however, knew that wherever the plaque that bore the British coat-of-arms sat, so sat the district seat, and refused to surrender their symbol of power. An equally determined mob from Elizabethtown descended upon Johnstown to remove the plaque. A pitched battle took place resulting in broken limbs and bloody noses, until the victorious Elizabethtowners carried the coat-of-arms back to its new home.

On a tract of land that had been generously donated by William Buell,[9] the town's founder, a New England-style courthouse square was laid out overlooking the river. There, a wooden courthouse with an adjoining jail was built. It was replaced in 1824 by a more substantial brick structure, which also quickly proved to be inadequate for the rapidly growing town. Meanwhile, the town had taken on a new name, Brockville.

In 1842, Toronto architect John Howard[10] designed a "Palladian" style courthouse for the growing community, and, in 1862–63, Kingston's Henry Horsey[11] developed plans to enlarge and improve the jail. When finished, the two-storey stone building consisted of a wing on the east end of the courthouse, with its entrance from within the court. The first floor of the jail contained ten criminal cells measuring two metres by one metre, while five debtor's cells on the second floor were double that size. In 1898, a two-storey residence to house the governor or jailer was added to the east end of the court. The jail remains

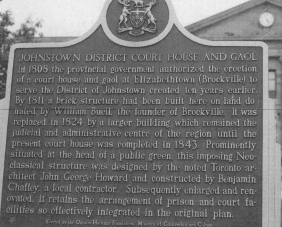

JOHNSTOWN DISTRICT COURT HOUSE AND GAOL
In 1808 the provincial government authorized the erection of a court house and gaol at Elizabethtown (Brockville) to serve the District of Johnstown created ten years earlier. By 1811 a brick structure had been built here on land donated by William Buell, the founder of Brockville. It was replaced in 1824 by a larger building which remained the judicial and administrative centre of the region until the present court house was completed in 1843. Prominently situated at the head of a public green, this imposing Neoclassical structure was designed by the noted Toronto architect John George Howard and constructed by Benjamin Chaffey, a local contractor. Subsequently enlarged and renovated, it retains the arrangement of prison and court facilities so effectively integrated in the original plan.
Erected by the Ontario Heritage Foundation, Ministry of Citizenship and Culture

*Above*, Brockville's jail and courthouse, visible behind the plaque, form part of a New England style courthouse square; *right*, the governor's house at the Brockville jail was added in 1898.

in use, surrounded by razor wire, and guarded by security cameras.

These security measures would have proven useful in 1876 when convicted murderers, brothers James and John Young made their daring escape. While the jailer was in James's cell making the prisoner's bed, the shackled Young beat him senseless with his leg irons, then lifted the key to free himself. Making his way upstairs, he released his brother. Together they fled over the low wooden wall and escaped down river. To prevent a recurrence, the government recommended that a separate residence be built for the jailer, and a more substantial stone wall be erected around the jail. Both recommendations were ultimately carried out.

Some of the punishments inflicted on the inmates of the time included solitary confinement and reduced diet. Otherwise, prisoners had a right to daily visits from friends and access to a priest or doctor. Debtor prisoners enjoyed a few extra "privileges" such as the ability to buy "wholesome plain food," fresh bedding and a pint of wine or a quart of beer.

Meanwhile, back at Johnstown, the original district town has almost vanished, the most prominent structure now being the looming bridge to the U.S.A. On the vacant site of the courthouse and jail, an historical plaque and prisoner's stock recall the former district seat and the battle for the coat-of-arms.

The original courthouse square remains overlooking Court House Avenue north of King Street in the heart of downtown Brockville.

## CAYUGA

There was a time when Cayuga, a town along the Grand River in what was then Haldimand County, was a much busier place than it is today. Part of a land grant to the Mohawk leader Joseph Brant, the village was developed in the 1930s as a transportation centre on the Grand River Canal. Two railways ultimately arrived, and Cayuga began to develop into a prosperous service centre. But a curse by a doomed prisoner in the county jail may have brought that promise to a shuddering halt.

In 1850, Cayuga was chosen as the capital for the newly created County of Haldimand, and accordingly a courthouse and jail were built. An addition to the rear of the courthouse, the jail mirrored the Greek-temple style on the front of the court building. At first the jail consisted of a two-storey central portion with single-storey wings to the sides. In 1877, these were converted to two storeys. This alteration was to allow windows to be placed in the original second-storey cells without risking prisoner escapes onto the roof below.

The 1877 renovations also added indoor toilets for each cell block. The second floor was reserved for female prisoners, with a death row cell as well. Placed right beside the fateful cell was the gallows, built into the structure to act as a permanent deterrent for both prisoners and public to see. Prior to 1877, the exercise yard was surrounded by only a plank fence, the weakness of which was demonstrated when two condemned inmates escaped only days before their scheduled execution. Following that embarrassment, the feeble wall was replaced with one of stone, that reached over five metres in height.

The most notorious of the executions which took place in the Cayuga jail was the twin hanging of two members of the dreaded Townsend Gang.[12] This seven-member mob had embarked upon a rampage of robberies and beatings, which culminated in the murder of a storekeeper at nearby Nelles Corners. After three were captured, one of the trio, William Bryson, decided to testify against the others, and was spared the death penalty. The other two, George King and John Blowes, were hanged before a public gallery of several thousand spectators. Blowes was buried in the yard after no one claimed his body. The gang leader, William Townsend, was never captured; the rest disappeared from history.

The courtyard at the now closed Haldimand County jail in Cayuga, the courtyard that Olive Sternaman could see from her cell window.

A later execution nearly went awry when the trap door refused to open. Several blows from a sledge hammer solved that problem. Another condemned man went to his death protesting his innocence all the way. His final words bestowed a curse upon Cayuga—that it would never grow or prosper beyond what it then was. Only after his execution was his innocence proven. Cayuga never grew after that.

Olive Sternaman, on the other hand, was acquitted of murder in 1898 even though it had been proven that two of her three husbands both died mysteriously shortly after taking out pricy insurance policies. Her pardon, however, only came as the result of hundreds of signed petitions, some from as far away as Toronto. From her cell window in the Cayuga jail, she could see the gallows being prepared for her hanging.[13]

While the courthouse was rebuilt in 1922 after a devastating fire, the original jailer's residence survived. It is an elegant two-storey Italianate house built of red and yellow brick, constructed during the jail renovations of 1877–78. In 1968, after the death of the last jailer, the parole board and the Ministry of Transportation moved their offices into the house. The jail itself was closed three years after that. Today the jailer's fine house contains additional courtroom space required by the attorney general's office.

The imposing governor's house at the county jail in Cayuga was built of red and yellow brick.

The building that housed the registry office, a component of the county building complex, has been enlarged to contain the county museum and archives. In addition to the extensive archival collection, the museum grounds also contain an 1835 pioneer log cabin. The entire complex looks out over the flowing waters of the Grand River, as it has for more than a century and a half. The site is located on Regional Road 54, north of Highway 3, on the northern periphery of the town.

## CHATHAM

It could be easy to overlook the City of Chatham (now part of the new Municipality of Chatham-Kent). The city lies off the main transportation corridors and there are very few major attractions within its urban boundaries to cause anyone to take much notice. That is not to say it is entirely without appeal. For one thing, it lies at the head of navigation on the Thames River, making it Ontario's only "inland" port. Its main street backs onto the water, presenting to the visitor an unusual juxtaposition of the downtown and the river. Its African-Canadian heritage is compelling,[14] and the city's museum-theatre complex has become a major regional arts focus. Unfortunately, Chatham has lost too many heritage buildings in recent years, all due to an absence of political will and foresight. But despite these losses, the city still retains its historic courthouse and jail, and these are significant, being among the oldest ones in Ontario.

By the 1840s Chatham had grown into a small but energetic mill town and inland port. Schooners and small steamers would made their way up the Thames River from Lake St. Clair to load their cargoes of barley and lumber. Development was quickly filling up the town plan, which had been created for it years earlier by John Graves Simcoe when he conceived of Chatham as being the site of a naval garrison.

However, being a port, the site attracted a robust criminal sector. In 1841, the town doctor reported a break and enter. According to him, the thief had removed the doctor's wallet and money from his pants. Although the doctor claimed to have identified the culprit, the charge was mysteriously dropped, and the chagrined medic was ordered to pay the accused $50 in retribution. In 1842, more break-ins netted thieves guns and whisky. In one case, a thief made off with an entire barrel of whisky. It would seem he must have been sampling it along the way as his footprints in the snow led from the crime scene directly to his hideout. So rampant was crime becoming that the *Chatham Journal* proposed a "society to entrap the thieves," further referring to them as "rowdies, swindlers and humbugs."

It took, however, until 1849 for the good citizens to welcome their new county jail. "The courthouse was for the lawyers," exclaimed a local wag, "while the jail was for the other rascals."[15] In 1847, when the Provisional District of Kent was created, the winning contract for the courthouse and jail went to architect William Thomas[16] of Toronto whose impressive resume included Toronto's Don Jail, and Guelph's City Hall. One of the stonemasons who worked on the walls would go on to become the second prime minister of Canada. His name was Alexander MacKenzie.

Prior to the completion of the courthouse and jail in Chatham, many of the area's judicial proceedings had taken place in Dawn Mills, a once thriving mill town on the Sydenham River some 40 kilometres north of Chatham. It has long since become a ghost town. The work on the courthouse began in 1847 and was completed in 1850. The first floor of the courthouse included a portion of the jail, which was incorporated into the back of the court. The complex was located well away

The now vacant Kent County courthouse in Chatham was designed by William
Thomas of Toronto.

from the centre of town, in a leftover gore, a triangular parcel of property lying between larger parcels of surveyed land, on what was then
the fringe of a residential area. But, by 1855, it was being criticized by
a grand jury for its lack of security and poor sanitation. And, by 1866,
the inspectors were recommending a "younger and more active jailer."[17] The expressed concerns would continue. In 1872, the ventilation
system came under fire. "Nearly every cell had defective ventilation
and the smell was unbearable...the absurd system of ventilation flows
between the cells and the corridor rather than to the outside."[18]

The jail recorded a rather unusual escape in 1884. One Peter Marks
had been left locked in the kitchen, but when the jailer returned he
was gone. The only explanation given was that he had managed to
squeeze through the bars in the top part of the kitchen door, bars
which were only 6 and 1/4 inches apart.

In 1943, the jail became the scene of an attempt to free two members of a notorious gang of bank robbers. On the night of September
9, four masked men barged into the home of the Royal Bank manager
in Wheatley, a fishing town 70 kilometres south of Chatham. There
they held him and his wife hostage through the night until the time
lock on the bank vault was released in the morning. The gang hastened
to the bank, tied up the bank employees, grabbed $35,000 and fled.
The robbers were caught in Windsor and brought back to the

Chatham jail to await trial. Two were released on bail while the other two remained incarcerated. On October 27, while making his rounds of the jail, the jail's governor, Phil Daigneau, surprised an intruder sitting atop the jail's outer wall. Below him was a car with its engine running. The intruder, equipped with ropes and revolvers, was caught trying to spring the two gang members. He would later be sentenced to 15 months in jail. In December, all four robbers were convicted and received sentences ranging from seven to fifteen years.

Over the years more improvements and additions were made to both the county building and jail. In 1981, the courthouse was declared a provincial heritage building, but due to the lack of handicap access, it was then closed. A new courthouse was opened, and the old building left vacant. In 2006, the jail remains in use, but the once active courthouse sits forlorn, waiting for a heritage saviour in a town that has had too few of them. The two buildings lie on the north side of Stanley Street, a block east of Adelaide Street in the eastern end of the city.

## COBOURG

If you stay overnight in the Cobourg jail, you just might see Henry the Ghost. At least, so the bartender might tell you. That's because the historic jail is not only part pub, part bed and breakfast, and part museum, but it may also be haunted. However, no one seems sure just who "Henry" was.

The fact that a jail was located in Cobourg in the first place originated with a tragic act of fate. Originally, in 1797, the district seat for Newcastle was placed at Presqu'ile Point, a long sandy spit stabbing into Lake Ontario about two kilometres farther east near Brighton. A townsite was laid out, and the courthouse and jail built. After its completion, the first criminal trial was set to take place. As no road had yet been opened to the new capital, the accused, the judge, the jurors and the various court officials climbed aboard a schooner named the *Speedy*. They set sail from the harbour at York (later Toronto) under darkening skies. But, as the *Speedy* rounded the point to enter the harbour, the squall bore down and swept the hapless vessel onto a shoal, sinking it with all on board.

With such a sudden and tragic loss of a large portion of its legal community, the government decided almost immediately to abandon the ill-fated location and chose instead a safer site. The new location was in Hamilton Township, several kilometres closer to York. Here on a hilltop, a wooden, combined courthouse and jail was erected. Gradually, stores, hotels and houses appeared around it and the community known as Amherst was born. (Today's location would be Burnham Road and Elgin Street in west-end Cobourg). This jail was replaced in 1832 by a more substantial structure built across the road, a building that in turn was replaced, in 1856, with a combined courthouse and jail. Three storeys high, the new facility contained 24 cells, along with a jailer's office and an isolation cell.

It was here, in 1859, that one of the province's most famous trials took place. In 1858, while his wife was convalescing from a fall, Dr. William King met and fell in love with Melinda Vandervort. While her husband courted the lovely Melinda, Mrs. King's condition mysteriously worsened, with vomiting and burning sensations in her stomach. In agony, she finally died. Her family, however, could not believe that she died of natural causes and requested that the body be examined. When arsenic was found in her stomach, Dr. King was arrested for murder. The jury found him guilty, and, although he continued to protest his innocence, King was sentenced to hang. Finally he published a confession in the Toronto *Globe*. On June 9, 1859, before a throng estimated at 10,000, William King was hanged. Afterwards, Melinda took on a series of other lovers before turning to alcohol. Ultimately declared insane, she died in an asylum.

It was from the Cobourg jail that a 12-year-old inmate escaped by prying the bars free with a bed rail and climbing down the wall, using his bedsheets, to support his weight.

Meanwhile, Cobourg itself was growing rapidly in a different location, near the harbour. In 1874, architect Kivas Tully of Toronto, born in Queens County, Ireland, set up his architectural offices in Toronto. He designed many government buildings, including county jails and the spectacular Victoria Hall[19] in the heart of Cobourg's main street. Once completed, the court facilities were transferred there. Then, in 1906, the old jail was also closed and a new one built behind a turn-of-the-century manor house near the new hall. The expansive red brick house was used to accommodate the jail's governor and the turnkey, while the cell block and exercise yard were built behind. There was also a chapel located at the rear of the second floor that, in

*Above*, Northumberland's county jail was incorporated into this existing manor house in Cobourg; *below*, one of the jail cells that has been adapted to a new use as a guest room in the King George Inn.

addition to being used for worship, also hosted staff meetings, parole meetings and sessions of Alcoholics Anonymous.

In 1998, this jail, too, was finally closed and converted into the present inn, pub and museum, known as the King George Inn. The tavern occupies most of the main floor of the house and guest rooms have taken over both the bedrooms and the upstairs cell blocks, while the former fingerprinting area is now one of the inn's lounges. The museum consists of the main floor cell block and the basement, where visitors can see the old cells, the medical room and many of the other functions found in early jails. The solitary confinement area and "bull pen" where prisoners were held upon arrival, have been left in their original form. The containment area still has carvings etched into the wall by the restless inmates. Tennis courts, badminton courts and basketball courts now occupy the jail's former exercise yard.

The earlier jail and courthouse became the Golden Plough Retirement Home and, in 1992, proposals were presented to convert it into a museum. However, when the later jail became available as a museum, these proposals were shelved. A new retirement home now occupies the original jail site.

Cobourg is blessed with many other historic attractions as well. The market building and Victoria Hall are directly across the road from the jail, and Victoria Park, with its beach and bandshell, lies a short distance further east. A few blocks away, the former Victoria College, and the Grand Trunk railway station, now a busy VIA Rail stop, add to the town's heritage treasure trove. The old jail faces Third Street, a block south of the imposing Victoria Hall.

## CORNWALL

The sturdy courthouse and jail in the eastern Ontario City of Cornwall are considered to be among Ontario's oldest public buildings, predated only by the 1825 courthouse in L'Orignal, a community on the Ottawa River about 60 kilometres east of Ottawa.

In 1788, the District of Lunenburg was created to administer the newly blossoming Loyalist settlements along the shore of the St. Lawrence River. In 1794, the government of Upper Canada ordered the construction of a courthouse and jail in both Johnstown, near Prescott, and New Johnstown,[20] the original name for Cornwall. Four years later, the log jail was complete and was followed, in 1802, by the two-storey wooden courthouse. The lower floor of the jail was divided into one room for the jailer, and two for the inmates while the upper floor was for the court and jury.

Early executions were usually public affairs. In 1820, one John Wilson from Glasgow was hanged for "high treason." There were two

The historic courthouse on Water Street in Cornwall. Note the prisoner's stocks on display in front of the building.

executioners, the first who hanged Wilson and the second who decapitated him, holding the head aloft to the crowd and proclaiming "Behold the head of a traitor." The following year four others were executed in public view for the murder of one John Sibert of Williamsburg.

But the first jail was utterly inadequate and prisoners often had to be removed from it to a "place of safety." Following a fire in 1826, which destroyed the original courthouse, a new courthouse and jail were built. During construction, a private home was altered to house a temporary jail. The new jail was extended in 1836 with a small stone structure being added to serve as a barracks for the 15th regiment who had arrived to quell brawling workers constructing the Cornwall Canal. Coming as they did from varying cultural backgrounds, the canal construction workers were notorious for getting into brawls at the slightest provocation. The jail contained 14 cells in each of the ground floor and basement, but lacked a fence.

Inspections in 1842 highlighted deficiencies in the new building. They noted that the jail "stank" for lack of a means of disposing the human waste. Debtors and criminals were separated as in most common jails, but the jail lacked separate facilities for women. Things improved somewhat in the 1850s with the addition of windows, a day room and a separate cell block for women. At this time a stone wall was erected around the exercise yard.

The courthouse was enlarged in 1886 and, in 1958, a new county building added. The jail continued to house inmates awaiting trial until 2002, when the Ministry of Correctional Services closed the facility. Stocks that once held criminals are on display, depicting what was once a humiliating and uncomfortable alterative to life inside the jail. The historic courthouse and jail can be found on the north side of Water Street at the corner of Pitt Street, overlooking the canal-side of Lamoureux Park. Today, the Historic Cornwall Jail is open to the public as a tourist attraction.

## GODERICH

Everything in Goderich, it seems, is at an odd angle. First, there is the main street. Laid out in an ancient Roman plan, the eight-sided "square" encompasses the town's business district and its courthouse. Some distance away the jail, too, is an octagon. And both, the town square and the jail, are well preserved.

Goderich was established on Lake Huron around 1828 as a focus for marketing land in the Huron Tract through settlement known as the Canada Company.[21] A settlement road, the Huron Road, was surveyed from Guelph to encourage settlers to establish farms in the area. Although the directors of the Canada Company had originally ordered that the name Goderich be applied to the first community established by their company, John Galt, the company commissioner, had already founded a village and had given it the name of Guelph, much to their chagrin. Hence, Goderich became the name of the new settlement at the mouth of the Maitland River.

At that time the district consisted of what are now the counties of Perth, Huron and Bruce. Goderich was its capital. As noted, in order to fulfill its obligations as the district seat, Goderich required a courthouse and jail. The first structures quickly proved inadequate and, in 1839, a new stone building was started. The eight-sided centre block was built of local stone and originally housed the court on the third floor. The jailer (or governor) lived in a small apartment on the second floor. Two cell blocks radiated from the central block; in them were twelve cells, nine for men and three for women. Designed by architect Thomas Young of Toronto, the jail was considered to be on the leading-edge of architecture for its time. It opened in 1842.

*Above*, the octagon jail in Goderich, designed by Thomas Young, is one of Ontario's better known jail museums, and was considered to be "state of the art" when it opened in 1842; *right*, this circular staircase led to the former courtroom in the Goderich jail.

A few design elements, however, did not work out too well. With the courtroom on the upper level, court magistrates had to pass by the cells of those prisoners whose cases they were considering. They objected to this imposition. Finally, the judges were driven out entirely by the smell of the human waste buried in the yard, immediately adjacent to the building. In addition, the residents of the town wanted the courthouse to be more centrally situated. As a result, in 1856, a new courthouse was opened in the centre of the square. It would burn in the fire of 1948 and be replaced.

In 1859, proper lavatories were added to the jail and, in 1861, the jailer moved into his own cabin in the exercise yard. Still, the accommodation for the jailer remained inadequate, being constantly cold and damp. Finally, in 1901, a large two-storey residence was built and connected directly to the main jail. It remained occupied by jail governors until 1968. The jail itself was closed four years later.

One of the jail's earliest guests was the notorious James Donnelly, patriarch of the "Black Donnellys." In 1857, he was charged with the murder of a local farmer near the village of Lucan, which was then a part of Huron County. Following his trial he was sent to the penitentiary in Kingston where he served seven years. In 1880, Donnelly, along with four other family members, was massacred in what was one of Ontario's grisliest and most publicized crimes.[22] Those widely publicized trials occurred in the Middlesex County courthouse in London, which by then had jurisdiction over the Lucan area.

One of the Goderich jail's last inmates was a 14-year-old named Steven Truscott who had been charged with the murder of a 12-year-old girl near Clinton in 1969. Originally sentenced to death, Truscott's sentence was converted to life in prison. Truscott, now free, has consistently denied any wrong-doing and has challenged the validity of those charges.[23]

A century earlier, the last public hanging in Huron, (some local material says likely in Canada,[24] occurred when Nicholas Maladay of Huron County was executed for the double murder of his father and step-mother. The last execution at the jail, a private one, was in 1911 when Edward Jardine dangled for the rape and murder of 12-year-old Lizzie Anderson. Although unable to witness the event, a crowd of 2,000 gathered at the jail entrance as the hanging took place.

Despite the high thick walls, and the sturdy steel doors, escapes did take place. In 1879, two inmates, who been jailed for two years, waited in the yard as a plank was hurtled over from outside. Quickly, they attached a string of sheets to the plank and tossed it back over, where their accomplices held it tight as the escapees pulled themselves up and over the wall. They were never to be seen again. Other aspiring fugitives were not so lucky. In 1880, after scaling the wall and jumping into a mound of snow, a hopeful fugitive fled into the frigid night, but returned when hunger and the bitter weather proved too much for him. In 1881, still another escapee managed to wedge sticks into the wall, forming a ladder which he used to reach the top of the wall. However, when his leap to freedom broke both legs, he was re-interred, painfully.

For the most part, however, inmates consisted of the poor, the homeless, and the insane. While poorhouses were frequently recommended to house the impoverished, the counties argued they didn't have enough money to build them.[25] Indeed a provincial inspection

report in 1875 noted that "the absence of crime in the populous county of Huron indicated by the entire absence of criminal prisoners is
most praiseworthy. Those in there were vagrants or insane."[26]

Finally, after 130 years of use, the jail was closed in 1972 and the prisoners transferred to the jails in Walkerton and Stratford. In 1974, the
building was opened as a museum, and the following year became a
national historic site. Today it is one of the area's major tourists attractions, and retains many of the facility's authentic features including the
cells, the kitchen, and the early jailer's apartment and office. A facsim-
ile of the first courtroom and the governor's residence have been real-
istically presented. In this case a visit to jail is a positive experience.

The old eight-sided stone jail lies on Highway 21 at the north end of
Goderich, overlooking the broad sweep of the Maitland River valley.

## GORE BAY

Far from the populous cities of southern Ontario, on the distant
shores of lore-filled Manitoulin Island, sits another of Ontario's most
authentic jailhouse museums—the one in Gore Bay.

By Ontario standards, Gore Bay is not that old. European settlement
began there around 1870 as a port of call for ships plying the North
Channel between Manitoulin and the mainland. As lumbering on the
island and farming on the island increased, Gore Bay expanded.
Because of its central location on the island's north shore, in 1889 it was
chosen as the district seat for Manitoulin District, freeing the inhabitants from the long journey to Sault Ste. Marie, the existing capital.

The jail and courthouse were designed by Kivas Tully, the government architect responsible for many of Ontario's government buildings from 1867 to 1901. The courthouse was designed as a two-storey
stone building with a front gable. Beside it was built the residence for
the crown attorney. Set separately from the courthouse, the jail consisted of a two-storey house for the jailer (not called a "governor" in
this case) that was attached directly to the cell blocks, which held a
total of ten cells. Here, women were housed on the second floor cell
block, men on the first. This configuration is known as a "Canadian
plan" jail.[27] To allow for some modesty, the women's cell doors had
bars for only the upper half, while those for the men had bars for the
full length.

The prisoners' table in the Gore Bay jail still retains the carvings etched into it by the inmates.

Throughout its 55-year life span, the jail housed primarily drunks and vagrants. In 1910, of 110 persons placed in the cells, more than 90 were charged with "drunk and disorderly." There was only one man sentenced to die there, and that was one Ed Cabino, who had shot his wife to death on near-by Cockburn Island. But because Cabino had been continuously beaten by his wife, who was twice his weight, the residents from as far away as Massey petitioned to have the sentence commuted to life in prison. In fact, Cabino was considered so harmless that the arresting constable declined to use handcuffs, and even took him home for breakfast before bringing him to the jail. The petition was successful, and Cabino spent the rest of his life in the Burwash Prison Farm near Sudbury.

The Manitoulin District jail in Gore Bay is now a museum.

There was also at least one escape from the sturdy jail. In 1915, Louis Shanawabin, in jail for horse theft, scaled the wall and headed for nearby Kagawong. Here, Constable Sandy Burns, caught up with him. Pretending not to know the fugitive, Burns asked him to hold his horse while he went into a nearby house for food. The hungry Shanawabin complied, only to discover too late he had been tricked and was taken back to Gore Bay where an extra six months was added to his sentence.

The jail was closed in 1945 and sat vacant for nearly a decade. At a time when heritage buildings were not regarded as highly as more recently, the far-sighted authorities and residents in Gore Bay succeeded in converting the jail into a museum. Today, it remains largely unaltered. Doors, windows and cell blocks all remain as they were when the last prisoners filed out. Even the inmates' dining table, complete with carvings, still stands before the cells. Because of its authenticity, and the fact that it is rare example (perhaps the only example) of a "Canadian plan" jail, efforts are under way to have it declared a national historic site. Meanwhile, court sessions are still being held in the adjacent courthouse. Beside it, the crown attorney's house rounds out the historic complex. All are located on a scenic hillside two blocks west of the village's main street.

## GUELPH

Guelph is one of Ontario's more fortunate cities. Spread over a scenic seven hills, it can boast of many surviving heritage structures. These include fountains, bridges, mills, hotels, churches, a railway station and government buildings, as well as an historic complex of county buildings, complete with the former jail.

When, in 1837, the District of Wellington was lopped off from the older District of Gore, whose seat at the time was in Hamilton, Guelph was selected as the new district seat. As part of its obligation to fulfill this status, the city had to build both a courthouse and jail. While the jail was ready in 1840, three more years would pass before the courthouse was completed.

The court building was constructed in a castle-like design. Located separately behind the courthouse, the jail was an octagonal structure, much like that which still stands in Goderich. Designed by Thomas Young, the jail was surrounded by a solid stone fence. Two other

Part of the original jail yard wall at the Wellington County jail in Guelph now encloses a landscaped garden.

buildings rounded out the justice complex—the crown attorney's office (25 Douglas Street), built of yellow brick in 1885, and the county solicitor's building (15 Douglas Street) an earlier stone structure, built in 1865. While the original courthouse and the two later buildings still stand, the jail was replaced in 1911. The new jail was built to replicate the courthouse, and stood two storeys high, topped off with a pair of crenellated towers. The governor's or jailer's house was added adjacent to it. Designed by a local architect named William Mahoney,[28] it was built using the stone from the original jail. Between them, the two jails witnessed a total of six executions, the first being a Charles Coghlin, hanged for murder in 1847, and the last James Giovenzzo, executed in 1919.

The newer county jail in Guelph was built in a style similar to the courthouse.

Escapes are always cause for alarm if not amusement. In 1876, while guarding eleven prisoners in the exercise yard, (or "airing" yard), the turnkey went to let a visitor out. While the jailer was thus distracted, one of the prisoners smashed the lock on the yard gate and made his escape.

By 1980 the jail, originally designed to house 28, had 55 inmates crammed into its tiny cells. When the Wellington Detention Centre was opened in that year, the old jail was closed. Along with the governor's residence, it was then extensively renovated to house some of the adjacent court facilities, including a law library. The exterior, however, has remained much as it originally appeared. While the interior is out of bounds to the public, portions of the stone wall that surrounded the 1840 exercise yard have been incorporated into the landscaping for a lawn and garden.

The courthouse fronts onto Woolwich Street, north of MacDonnell Street and south of Eramosa Road. The former jail and governor's house lie behind it. Access to it and the landscaped grounds are from Douglas Street. The historic downtown core of Guelph lies a block to the west.

## KITCHENER

From the time that Kitchener still was known by its original name of Berlin, the Waterloo County jail has stood. Today, it is one of Ontario's oldest surviving jail buildings.

Waterloo County was once part of the District of York, with the court and jail located in the distant Town of York. In 1816, when the District of Gore was severed from York and included today's Waterloo County, a new jail and courthouse were built, this time in Hamilton. At that time the jail was in the lower level of a two-storey log courthouse. While this was closer to the inhabitants of Berlin, it was still a long distance to travel to achieve justice. Then, in 1838, with the creation of yet another new district, that of Wellington, the new jail and court came closer still, and were built in Guelph.

Finally, in 1852, the Berliners got their wish, and today's Waterloo County came into being. The two-storey stone jail, designed by Mellish and Russell of Brantford, was opened a year later.[29] At first the jail contained fourteen single cells and six double cells, but had no wall. The following year a wooden fence was built to enclose the airing yard, while ten iron window grates were installed in the jail building

The Waterloo County jail in Kitchener is now part of the new courthouse.

itself. Overcrowding was an almost instant problem, with thirty-eight men and one woman being crammed into the cells in 1853. Among their crimes were theft of bees, swearing and disobeying a "master." Within the next five years improvements included more locks, plaster on the walls and new water closets. In the 1860s, the wooden fence was replaced with a more secure stone wall, five metres in height. In 1878, a residence was added to accommodate the new governor, Jonathan Cook. It was built in an Italianate style of red brick with yellow brick trim and included a grey marble fireplace mantel. Indoor plumbing and electricity were added to the jail in 1893.

Despite the stone wall, as with most Ontario jails, escapes were commonplace. In 1882, a prisoner named Haywood escaped the yard by piling several buckets on top of a bench. He then fled through the gate door, which the turnkey had left unlocked while he went to Sunday School.

Despite the improvements, in 1899, the prisoners were put to work breaking rocks, not just to defray costs (rocks were paid for by local builders), but "to drive away tramps to other counties."[30] As tramps often showed up just for free lodging and food, it was believed that the prospect of hard labour would discourage them. Convicts were also sent out to toil in the city's dusty factories and many of Kitchener's industries benefited from such cheap convict labour.

During the jail's operation, only three executions took place: those of James Allison in 1898, Stoyko Boyeff in 1920 and the last, that of

Reginald White in 1940. All were interred in the prison yard, according to the usual practice; unless next of kin claimed the body, it was buried there. While the remains of the first two were recovered during renovation and re-interred, White's body still lies somewhere under the parking lot that now occupies the yard area.

In 1931, the jail's first major addition increased capacity from 26 to 41 inmates. Yet even with modernization, the jail in 1977 was scathingly described by a grand jury as being "the black hole of Calcutta."[31] A year later, after 125 years of continuous operation, the jail was closed. And, in 1981, it was designated as a "Heritage Structure" by the City of Kitchener-Waterloo and studies to find alternate uses began. One of Ontario's most prolific restoration architects, Carlos Ventin,[32] was hired to do the job. Argentine-born, he gained his reputation when he was hired to conduct the demolition of the courthouse and jail in Simcoe, Ontario. Instead, he convinced the local council that they would save both money and a valuable heritage treasure by renovating rather than removing. He went on the help save the jails in both Woodstock and Milton as well.

Although the original courthouse, once located beside the jail, was demolished years earlier and replaced with a more modern building, the former jail still stands and now houses additional office space for the court and police. The lobby area, the only public area, contains artifacts found while restoration was taking place, including a key ring, handcuffs and the prisoner's dock from the original courthouse. Several early photographs line the lobby walls and show the jail as it appeared in its early years.

The former jail faces onto Queen Street, a block east of Weber Street, on the periphery of downtown Kitchener.

## LINDSAY

One of the most distinctive and strikingly beautiful jails (at least from the outside) is that at Lindsay, and its future is in safe hands.

In 1861, the County of Victoria was created from the United Counties of Lindsay and Peterborough, which in turn had been part of the Colborne District. The necessary courthouse, registry office and jail were finished two years later and opened for business. Like the jails in Woodstock, Gore Bay and St. Catharines (demolished), the one in

The Victoria County jail in Lindsay has become a museum.

Lindsay was an architectural treasure in its own right. Built separately from the courthouse, it faced directly onto Victoria Street. Italianate in design, the jail stood three storeys high and boasted an arched portico. Designed by Toronto architect James Storm, it was built using white brick and local limestone. Two wings of three bays each flanked the setback central portion. Single storey wings were added at a later date.

The front section was used by the jailer and turnkey for their accommodation, while the prisoners had to make do with cell blocks of six cells each, most of them barely wide enough to hold a cot. Early photos show a prison yard surrounded by a simple wooden fence. It was later replaced with a higher stone enclosure after a reporter won a bet with the jailer that he could escape by simply running at the wall and scaling a downspout.

While it is known that at least four executions took place here, the records of the unfortunate souls have been lost. It is known, however, that the first hanging took place on January 1, 1874. Like many a murder, it involved a love affair. The accused was a 35-year-old drifter who had travelled widely before settling in Lindsay to become a well-respected carpenter. There he fell in love with a married woman two years his senior. After moving in with the woman, he asked her to marry him. When she rejected him, the spurned lover shot her. Despite protesting his innocence, the perpetrator was convicted. She, he claimed, had shot herself, and complained that the witnesses had lied at his trail. Unlike earlier hangings elsewhere, this one was not to be public. Still the curious crowds swarmed the jail, even climbing onto the roof of a nearby church in hopes of glimpsing the grisly scene. The body was later buried beneath the scaffold.

In another instance, in 1877, the local citizenry had grown impatient with the inaction by the police against the multitude of brothels in the town. Frustrated, a vigilante group stormed through the town, burning as many of the "sin palaces" as they could reach. It was later alleged that the hesitancy by the constabulary was at least in part because the chief was a regular customer.

The jail fulfilled its function until 2002 when it was closed and the prisoners transferred to a controversial new super jail. But rather than being faced with demolition, such as happened with the St. Catharines jail, the building was declared a heritage site, and leased to the local historical society. Here, in conjunction with a number of other community groups, the society began to create a museum and a heritage and arts centre. While the tiny cells remain in place, the former quarters of the jailer and turnkey were earlier converted into an infirmary and staff room. Although the gallows and cemetery have long since been removed, the "death cell" with its rounded corners still remains visible. According to the historical society, these corners were designed so that the prisoner could not conceal himself from view through the small cell door opening.

The jail faces Victoria Street, five blocks north of Kent Street. Happily, the courthouse still survives just around the corner, giving the town a distinctive heritage complex.

## LONDON

Were it not for a last minute change of mind by Upper Canada's first administrator, John Graves Simcoe, London might have become the province's capital, rather than York, which later became Toronto.

As a result, London's growth was delayed and it was not until 1826 that it was designated a district seat. Thanks to the influence of Colonel Thomas Talbot, a prominent local land colonizer, the courthouse was designed to replicate his ancestral home, Castle Malahide in Ireland. Indeed, its four tall castellated towers give it an uncanny resemblance to a medieval European castle. And it came complete with "dungeons."

The Middlesex County jail in London saw a number of notorious convicts. The white castle-like courthouse is to the left, with the newer brick jail in the foreground.

Or at least that's what many observers had to say about the jail located in the basement. It was damp, poorly ventilated and badly drained, so much so that the smell of human excrement often permeated the courthouse above. At least one judge was so offended by the aroma that he moved the entire court proceedings outside. The execution of one of Ontario's worst mass murderers took place in this early jail. Convicted of the killing of his wife and six of his seven children, Henry Sovereene of Delhi was hanged here on August 13, 1832.

Finally, in 1846, a new jail was built on the west end of the courthouse. The two buildings could not have been more different in style. While the tall white castle-like courthouse loomed on the east end, the much simpler two-storey brick jail spread out below, its only embellishment a slender cupola above.

Conditions, however, did not seem to improve. Inspection reports in 1875 and 1876 complained that "the stench of the water closet pervaded every area…" and "Vermin are so numerous that the prisoners beg not to be locked in their cells as they are literally devoured in them."[33]

Over its century and a half of existence, the jail and its predecessor have housed some of Ontario's most famous prisoners. In 1838, 44 instigators of the "Windsor Raid"[34] were incarcerated. Six were found guilty of treason and hanged in front of the courthouse while the remainder were transported to the distant penal colonies in Australia.

One of the condemned, Joshua G. Doan of Sparta, Ontario, wrote a last letter to his wife, "I am confined to the cell from which I go to the gallows…Think as little of my unhappy fate as you can…may God protect you and my dear child."[35]

The first execution in London, which took place in 1830, was considerably more bizarre, as the condemned man, one Cornelius Burleigh, was hanged not once, but, after the rope broke on the first try, twice. At a time when London's population was only 300, the throng of onlookers was estimated at 3,000. Following his demise, Burleigh's body was promptly dissected by medical students, and his head removed. Years later the skull was returned and placed on display at the Eldon House Museum on Ridout Street in London.

Then, in 1880, the jail became home to one James Carroll, charged with being the ringleader of the vigilante gang that carried out the midnight massacre of five members of the hated Donnelly family of Lucan. It was a trial which attracted reporters from around the world. The first trial ended with a hung jury. Several months later the reporters returned for the second trial at which time the jury acquitted the defendant, after the judge was allegedly ordered by political higher-ups to make sure that Carroll was let go.[36] There was, it seems, an election pending, and the politicians were accused of not wanting to discourage the local Irish vote by having Carroll convicted.

In fact, many of the Donnellys themselves became familiar guests in the London jail on charges that ranged from assault to arson. However, many lesser-known inmates made their home here too. Another early suspect, who had blamed Indians for the murder of his wife and six children, was convicted after a clump of his hair was found clenched in his wife's hand. The only time a woman was hanged was in 1872 when one Phoebe Campbell, who had murdered her husband in order to continue an affair with her hired hand, was put to death. The jail's last execution occurred in 1951 when Walter Rowe and Russell Bechard of Detroit were hanged for the murder of a bystander while they were trying to rob a taxi driver. They claimed they did not know the gun was loaded. The jury, understandably, was not convinced. The jail continued to offer its grim accommodation until 1974 when it was at last closed. The courthouse was converted to a county administration building with the second floor courtroom becoming the county council chambers.

During the years which followed, funds were raised by the county and local citizens to save the jail portion as well. The 1ˢᵗ Hussars, the regiment that began as the London Volunteer Cavalry in 1856 and renamed as the 1ˢᵗ Hussars in 1892. (They sent troops to fight in the Boer War and both World Wars.) The museum was moved into the basement, where a cell block has been preserved to show to modern society the cruel conditions that awaited prisoners even up to "enlightened" times. Here eight cells, each measuring a mere two and a half metres (about eight feet by three feet) show how confined the conditions were. Here, too, is the isolation cell, a tiny totally darkened closet where those who disturbed the "peace" or who talked back to the guards were placed for up to 24 hours. It is among these dark cells that the ghost of Marion "Peg Leg" Brown, hanged in 1899 for the murder of a London police constable, is said to still wander.

The courthouse and jail museum overlook the Thames River in downtown London, at the historic corner of Ridout and Dundas streets.

## L'ORIGNAL

The name of this scenic eastern Ontario community, located near present-day Hawkesbury on the Ottawa River, will not sound familiar to many Ontarians. Yet, it has served as a district and later county seat for what is now Prescott and Russell County longer than any other town in the province. And its courthouse is Ontario's oldest.

In 1674, France created the Seigneury of L'Orignal on the south shore of the Ottawa River. This swampy lowland remained undeveloped until 1796 when Nathaniel Treadwell purchased the site and built mills and roads. In 1816, when the District of Ottawa was formed, L'Orignal became its district seat. But judicial facilities remained crude. The first court sessions were held in the schoolhouse, while the sheriff's house served as the jail. Punishment was primitive as well—a man convicted of stealing flour was given 39 lashes.

From 1819 to 1829, construction crews arrived to build the Grenville Canal designed to bypass a set of furious rapids on the Ottawa River. The waterway soon bustled with small boats. A road was laid along the river's shore, linking L'Orignal with Pointe Fortune and soon stagecoaches began to rattle their way through the village as well. But despite the activity and its municipal stature, the town remained small.

L'Orignal's jail sits beside Ontario's oldest courthouse.

Finally, a grand new courthouse was opened in 1825 to replace the woefully inadequate original structure. The jail was situated in the ground floor, a debtors' cell lay to the right of the entrance and the jailer's apartment and bedroom were to the left. At the rear of the central corridor, a small cell was located on the left and a larger criminals' ward on the right. A grand jury report in 1838 could find little good to say about the first jail—the door in the criminal's room was inadequate, as were the doors and windows in the women's cell and the debtor's room. Even the window in what the jury referred to as "the black hole" (the isolation cell) was not up to standard. As early as 1840, plans for a new jail were being presented by Sheriff Treadwell, but no action was taken.

As with many early jails, the one at L'Orignal was used to house both the criminal and the insane, such as a man who, in 1839, had to be kept constantly chained and handcuffed. Prior to the 1850s criminals were frequently punished by being placed on public view, their head and arms clamped in stocks located next to the courthouse. Being constrained in a wooden frame with holes for head and arms, was considered a form of public humiliation.

As result of province-wide jail reforms in 1857, a new jail was built adjoining the southeast end of the courthouse. The plans were devised by William Lundrum, the county jailer, using specifications drawn up by the Board of Prison Inspectors. The front portion of the new two-storey jail contained the jailer's home while the rear portion contained cell blocks on each of the two floors, with three large cells and six small cells on each level. There were to be, however, no indoor privies. Although the new jail was finished in 1862, the prison inspectors continued to find many faults including leaky roofs and poor security. Most of the repairs however were completed by 1868.

Over the following years, jail inspectors recommended a number of small repairs and on one occasion criticized the jailer for leaving the door unlocked, which allowed an inmate to escape. In 1874, the inspector was distressed to observe that a cell "occupied by a lunatic had no bedding save straw on the floor…it was very dirty and the air very foul. The jailer," noted the inspector, "stated that he was occasionally very violent and destroyed his bedding and everything else in the cell."[37] But the inspector dismissed this excuse, and ordered the jailer to place the madman in a clean cell. He also chastised the jailer for not keeping a pair of condemned prisoners "in the condition of confinement and isolation which is required…they were to be strictly confined to their cells…and a special guard was to be placed over them day and night."[38]

Escapes plagued the L'Orignal jail as they did everywhere. The inspector discovered that one escapee, upon being allowed into the yard to use the privy, scaled the high stone wall where the pointing was defective.

In 1905, electric lights were installed in the jail and eventually heating and indoor plumbing as well, but it took until 1930 for bathing facilities to be added. Later on, modern showers, a kitchen and telephones were installed as well. One prisoner attempted to use the phone to make a threatening call, but unaware that his calls were being recorded and traced, was quickly found out. Later on, the jail also offered a laundry, chaplaincy and school. One particularly large cell contained its own bathtub.

While the much enlarged courthouse still functions, and now includes the county and municipal offices, the jail was finally closed in 1998, and sits undisturbed. Although it was later used as the location for a film, "Francoeur," no further proposals for re-use have been finalized.

Aside from the historic courthouse and jail, the village retains much of its early authenticity. Court Street, which leads up to the front of the original courthouse, retains the former "Hotel de Ville" or town hall, now converted to court uses, as well as the former registry office. The town is scenically situated on the Ottawa River with many 19th century homes lining its quiet streets. L'Orignal lies eight kilometres west of Hawkesbury, a short distance north of Highway 417 in eastern Ontario.

## MILTON

Milton began in 1821, as a mill town, as did so many other Ontario towns. First named Martin's Mills, it had grown to a mere 100 persons by 1837. When the County of Halton separated from Wentworth in 1853, the question, as usual, was where to put the county buildings. While Oakville was the more logical location, being larger and more economically advanced, the provisional council had already made up its mind—it would be in Milton. This location, they concluded, was more central to the new county.

By 1855 the county buildings were opened. Resembling a medieval castle complete with two castellated towers, they sat facing a pasture, which would later become the town's Victoria Park. Even though Milton still lacked railway connections, and the roads were wretched, the additional functions supported by the courthouse, its employees and the supporting shops in town brought an unprecedented growth.

The first jail, however, was quickly proving to be unsatisfactory. In his 1876 report, the provincial inspector complained that the "condition of things are in violation of prison discipline...ventilation of the lower ward is exceedingly defective and yard space is insecure...the opening is so close to the angles of the walls as to affect an easy means of scaling."[39] In 1877, a new jail and exercise yard were added to the north side of the courthouse, and a registry office was located to the south.

The first of the town's three executions took place in 1858 with the hanging of Thomas Corner for the shooting of his wife and niece. Despite petitions pleading for a commutation, Corner was hanged in front of a large crowd that filled the future park area across from the courthouse door. The second hanging, also public, was that of a young boy who had beaten his mother to death while both were in a drunken stupor. Despite his best efforts, the sheriff, Levi Wilson, who had questioned the fairness of the trial, was unable to have the sentence commuted to imprisonment and the young boy, too, was hanged. Following the grim spectacle, Sheriff Wilson resigned in disgust.

The Halton County jail in Milton is now home to its municipal offices.

The final execution was held in 1883 in the new jail yard, out of the public's view. It involved a man named Michael O'Rourke who had been convicted of murdering an elderly Burlington man and his daughter. The difficulty with this execution was that there was not a hangman to be found in the region. Eventually, for $50, one was lured from Buffalo, New York. All three bodies were buried in the jail yard, unmarked and forgotten. Then, in 1979, when restoration work was set to begin, the remains were discovered and re-interred.

The jail consisted of a two-storey wing that extended east from the jail administration offices. It consisted of two cell blocks of six cells on each of the two floors. The jail offices and entrance were designed in a gothic style. Although the main tower is now gone, four smaller towers still penetrate the roof line.

The jail was closed in 1977, and, three years later, a far-sighted municipal council voted to preserve the complex and begin restoration. During the renovation, the interior was totally redone so that no trace of the cells remain. The buildings now house the town's municipal offices, while the walls of the exercise yard now enclose an attractive garden. The registry office has been enlarged to become a meeting hall. Meanwhile the governor's house still survives on the southeast side of the parking lot, serving as a place for the municipal offices.

Milton's heritage pride can be seen everywhere in town. The main street has been revitalized, and the former town hall now contains private offices. But the main focus of the town's heritage remains the courthouse and jail, which can be found on Brown Street, two blocks south of Main Street.

## NAPANEE

Napanee is one of those towns with a history that dates back to the earliest days of pioneer settlement in Upper Canada, and is one that has preserved and celebrated much of that heritage. Among its historic treasures are the red stone post office, the town hall with its market square, and its early stone Grand Trunk Railway station. It should come as little surprise then that its grand courthouse and county jail rank among its most treasured historic sites.

Since 1841 Kingston had been the government seat of the United Counties of Frontenac, Lennox and Addington, with the courthouse and jail being located there. In 1863, Lennox and Addington became a separate county and were allocated $20,000 to build a new courthouse and jail.

The Lennox and Addington County jail in Napanee is now the county's museum and archives.

Designed by architect John Power, the jail was completed by December of 1865 although that building alone had consumed most of the allocation. The walls were constructed of local limestone nearly a metre thick and five metres high. The two-storey cell block contained nine cells per floor, with six for men and three for women. The men's cells measured 2.5 metres by 3.2 metres, while the more generous women's cells were double that width. With no windows in the cells, the only illumination came from the openings on the outside walls of the blocks. On the south end of the structure stood a large two-storey house for the governor and his family. A pair of peep holes strategically placed in his home, allowed him to view each floor of the cell block corridors. Outside the building separate exercise yards were set aside for the two sexes.

While the jailers were paid by the county, the supply of food was let out by contract to local grocers in the town. Meals consisted of little more than bread, potatoes and meat with no provision for fruit or vegetables. Each cell was provided with a mattress sheet and night bucket, and the prisoners with uniforms. Bathing facilities, however, were sadly lacking, with prisoners being required to bathe in the kitchen located in the basement. Even as late as 1935, inspection reports complained that, "It is not satisfactory to bathe and cook in the same room." Until 1909, toilets were simply stone latrines in the exercise yards. In that year flush toilets were finally installed inside, more than a decade after the county had agreed to do so.

As with most local jails in 19th century Ontario, few inmates could be called criminals. In 1891, only seven of forty-four inmates had been charged with a criminal offence. While most of the chargeable offences were for things like assault and vagrancy, a few stood out, such as the farmer sentenced to four years for killing a cow, and a young woman, sentenced for illegally procuring a miscarriage.

Vagrancy was often an euphemism for prostitution and it was not unusual for these young women to have their children incarcerated with them. In the winter of 1881, of the fifteen inmates, six were young women, another six were children. One 16-year-old girl was sentenced no fewer than six times in a two-year period for vagrancy. But even she was not the youngest as two young boys, aged 10 and 12, served time for vagrancy and larceny respectively. In 1880, one Charles McGuin, penniless, sick and unable to consume anything other than fluids, was jailed for "vagrancy." He died soon after.

Although the jail held a gallows, no executions ever occurred. While five convicts were sentenced to die, all had their sentences commuted to life. There were, however, at least 25 escapes from the jail. A few fled before a proper turnkey was hired and another one before walls were erected. Some managed to use planks left lying around to scale the walls, while another, who had found civilian clothes in the kitchen, also lucked upon a ladder left in the yard and disappeared over the wall.

But perhaps the most bizarre escape not just from Napanee, but from possibly any county jail, was that by James Walker in 1930. While awaiting trial for a string of robberies, the determined Walker removed bolts from the crossbar of the door that led to the exercise yard and fled. Recaptured, he was locked in his cell and placed under close guard. When the guard went into

Little evidence, other than this cell, remain of jail days in the Napanee museum.

the cell to awake him on the day of his trial, he found a dummy under the bed sheet. According to the local newspaper, what little evidence there was seems to indicate that Walker had wrenched a piece of bracket from his radiator and, while clinging to the bars of his window, chipped his way onto the roof. Then, using blankets and a towel, he lowered himself to the ground and disappeared from the records.

In 1974, the jail was closed and two years later extensively renovated, becoming the county archives and museum. While nothing of the jail's interior remains intact, the governor's house, some of the walls, and the vaulted ceilings remain to recall its long legacy in this historic town. To help visitors better appreciate this heritage, the museum has published a detailed booklet *Behind the Limestone Walls* (authored by James Eadie), which recounts not just stories of the Napanee jail but reveals information on the county jail system across Ontario.

The jail is located behind the beautiful courthouse (still a county building) on Thomas Street, two blocks north of Dundas Street, the main street, and three blocks east of Centre Street, which is the Highway 41 entrance to town from the 401.

## OTTAWA

It is easy to overlook Ottawa's historic jail. With the city's incredible treasure trove of heritage buildings—the parliament buildings, the railway station (now a convention hall), historic hotels like the Château Laurier and the Elgin, Rideau Hall, 24 Sussex, and the list goes on, the old Ottawa jail seldom appears on the list of must-sees. Yet it remains one of the best preserved, and most dungeon-like, of Ontario's many heritage jails. It was built in 1862 to replace a combined courthouse and jail, which proved to be so inadequate that one prisoner simply dug through the wall to his freedom.

Like most, this jail, along with the courthouse had been erected in 1842 to satisfy the demands of Carleton County's new status as a county seat. Prior to that, Bytown's (as Ottawa[40] was then called) felons had to traipse to faraway Perth for their trial and possible incarceration. Ottawa's jail consisted of the governor's house, which faces onto

The Carleton County jail in Ottawa is little known, relative to the city's many other heritage attractions.

The range of cells in the Carleton County jail.

Nicholas Street, with the two floors of cell blocks behind. At the time of its opening, it was widely hailed as "a splendid building capable of holding 100 prisoners and is complete in all its parts. It is the model jail of Canada."[41]

Yet the dismal cells were barely a metre wide and completely lacked windows and ventilation. The cell block windows contained no glass, and over the years many prisoners simply froze to death. Nor did the cell block have ventilation, heat or running water. An inspection report in 1884 lamented that the one-inch water pipes were inadequate to flush the water closets, that there was a lack of bedsteads and that a female prisoner was being badly mistreated. The same report recounted that one escape attempt was carried out using a wooden key, while other escape devices were found hidden in the wooden window sills. The inspector immediately called for replacement of the sills.

The jail could also boast of having held Canada's last public hanging according to Corrections Canada, when, in 1869, Patrick James Whelan was hanged for the murder of Thomas D'Arcy McGee,[42] one of the Fathers of Confederation. A crowd of 5,000 gathered to watch. Two other death sentences over the years included that of Eugene Larment for the murder of police detective Thomas Stoneman. After having robbed the war museum of a collection of machine guns and pistols, Stoneman shot

The site of the gallows is still visible in Ottawa's Carleton County jail.

the detective near Slater and O'Connor streets. He claimed to be "not guilty" by reason of intoxication. In 1933, William George Seabrooke was hanged for the murder of a gas station attendant. This would be the jail's last execution. Finally, in 1972, described as a "medieval dungeon," mercifully, the Ottawa jail was closed.

Today, the building has been converted to a youth hostel, yet little has been changed inside. The cells remain as the former inmates might remember them, as do the narrow iron stairs and the sturdy doors that guard the cell blocks. Indeed, even the location of the gallows rests undisturbed. While the facility is not generally open to the public, guided tours are occasionally offered.

The courthouse, too, still survives a short distance north of the jail, as does the registry office, thus forming a complete heritage county building complex. The jail faces onto Nicholas Street beside the MacKenzie King Bridge on the east side of the Rideau Canal.

## OWEN SOUND

It is said that the Owen Sound jail and courthouse bore witness to one of Ontario's most grisly murder trials outside of that of the Black Donnelly's of Lucan fame.

It began, as do many, over the love of a lady. The damsel in question was one Ellen McCleary who lived a short distance from John A. Bailey. Estranged from his first wife, he had moved to a farm in Keppel Township, a short distance from Owen Sound. While there, he hired Ellen McCleary, a young woman from a nearby farm, to cook for him. As they came to know each other, Bailey fell in love with Ellen.

But he was not her only suitor. A frequent visitor, James King, fell for her as well, and both men asked her to marry them. Words were exchanged between Bailey and King, with Bailey challenging King to a fight. But King failed to show up. Instead, a week later, he and a friend arrived at Bailey's home while he was away, and waited for him. Taken by surprise, Bailey was an easy victim and was killed by a blow to the head. A hired man, who was living there at the time, was also killed. The house was then set ablaze and the bodies burned beyond recognition.

While investigating the mysterious deaths, a detective disguised himself as a traveling salesman and talked the lovely Ellen into a tryst in Palmerston, where he, and another detective in hiding, heard her confess that she and King had plotted the murder all along. However, at the trial, both denied the allegations, and in the absence of other witnesses, were freed. The year was 1886, and had followed on the heels of the widely covered trials of the Donnelly massacre in which the accused was also set free. One murder that did end in conviction was that of a blind man named Cook Teets who was convicted of poisoning his wife. He was hanged in 1884, the first execution to occur in the Owen Sound jail.

The building had been finished in 1853, shortly after the new County of Grey was created from the larger County of Wellington. Owen Sound had been chosen as the county seat over its chief rival, Durham.

The jail was constructed of orange limestone and was located right behind the courthouse. In later years, a governor's house was added to the north of the courthouse.

The jail's first escape occurred while it was still under construction. Greenaway Steele and his mother Martha Wall were placed in the jail to await transfer to the penitentiary at Kingston. As the scaffolding was still in place to build the wall, the pair climbed to the windows where friends had pried off the bars, and they fled. In fact, the jail gained something of a reputation for its escapes, as noted in Smith's *Gazetteer* of 1866. The jail, he noted, has "become a proverb in the County as scarcely a year passes but

The entrance to the Grey County jail in Owen Sound as seen from the courthouse.

The former courtroom in the Grey County courthouse is now a theatre.

some prisoner escapes."[43] Nor did that reputation diminish with time. In 1981, a 17-year-old fled simply by climbing the fire escape to the roof, and, in 1987, the prisoners formed a human pyramid to allow two others to escape by climbing down a bedsheet.

The jail could accommodate forty-eight men and four women at a time. The cells measured one metre by two-and-a-half metres, with arched ceilings. The facility was likened to "something from the Dark Ages" by a grand jury.

Although the jail was still in use in late 2003, the courthouse had been turned over to the city in 1985 for use as an arts centre, with the former courtroom used for theatrical productions. It would be interesting to see a theatrical production of the Bailey murder and trial, much the way the Donnelly massacre has been the subject of many such productions.

The historic former courthouse and adjacent jail are on 3rd Street East, between 12th and 13th streets. Close by are other historic features such as the harbour and the marine museum located in the former CN railway station.

## PARRY SOUND

Despite its small size and relative isolation, Parry Sound and its jail witnessed one of Ontario's most widely covered murder trials of the early 20th century. It had all the classic elements of a Capone-era crime including a daring train robbery, a midnight shootout, and a questionable execution.

It all began on August 18, 1928, when two (some say three) masked men smashed their way into the mail car of a moving CPR train near Sudbury, Ontario. As the train slowed to enter Parry Sound, the robbers slipped into the darkness. Near the station, the Laird brothers, Haughton and Walter, were startled from their sleep by the motor of their neighbour's car. Assuming correctly that it was being stolen, they hopped into their own car and took off in pursuit.

The darkened roads through the Parry Sound bush were narrow and winding. Near the village of Waubamik, they came upon the stolen car stuck in a ditch. A local farmer named Thomas Jackson and his son were working to free the vehicle when the Laird brothers approached the thief, pretending to have a gun. As the thief bolted from the car, shots rang out and Jackson crumbled from a bullet in his neck. Shortly afterward he died. The Lairds meanwhile had knocked the culprit, one John Burowski, unconscious and held him until the constable arrived. The other robber escaped into the darkness.[44]

He was sent to Toronto to await his trial, which would be held in Parry Sound. Meanwhile, the Parry Sound Police and the OPP searched desperately for the other train robber, or robbers. Despite filling the jail's 22 cells with upwards of 50 vagrants, none proved to be a fugitive. Finally, the unfortunate Burowski was returned by train to Parry Sound where the trial began. But this was the Capone period and the colourful Parry Sound murder had captured the attention of a crime-crazed public. Reporters from across Canada crowded into the courtroom. A mere three days after it began, the trial was over; Burowski was convicted and would be hanged at the Parry Sound jail. Shortly after midnight on December 22, the grisly sentence was carried out.

But many questions were raised. Why had the other robber or robbers not been more actively sought, especially after Burowski had named them? Moreover, no one had actually seen Burowski point the gun at Jackson. In fact, there was no evidence that it was even Burowski's gun that had killed the farmer. The trial had captured the attention of the nation, and had briefly put the town and its jail on the map. Indeed, the case led to a book, *Murder and Mayhem at Waubamik*, written by a local newspaper reporter some 75 years later.

This brick building represents the entrance to the district jail in Parry Sound.

Parry Sound's first jail and court were built in 1871 shortly after Parry Sound District had separated from the District of Muskoka. However, the clapboard structure proved inadequate and was replaced in 1878 by a separate jail, leaving the original wooden building solely as the courthouse. But this building, too, was altered in 1889 with a two-storey brick addition to the front.

Then, in 1901, the jail gained twelve new cells, men's and women's hospital rooms and a new day room. In 1905, a jailer's residence was added, while further additions two years later brought a new turnkey's room, another two-storey wing and more cells. More modernization took place in the 1970s and '90s as well.

While the jail is now closed, the courthouse remains in use. In 1903, a newspaper headline read, "For the first time within recollection the edifice is free of prisoners...this speaks well of this new and large district."[45] The same could be said 100 years later, but for a different reason.

Today, the courthouse, with the jailer's residence beside it and the cell blocks behind, dominates James Street, Parry Sound's main street, at the north end of the shopping district.

## PERTH

Few would quarrel that Perth ranks among Ontario's prettiest and most historic towns. The settlement can trace it roots back to the time of the War of 1812–14 between Canada and the United States. Concerned with the vulnerability of the Loyalist settlements along the St. Lawrence River and Lake Ontario shorelines, the British government ordered the surveying of a trio of military towns further inland—Richmond, Franktown and Perth. As half-pay officers of the British army and Scottish immigrants from the Lowlands around Glasgow made their way inland, Perth began to grow.

Being the seat of Bathurst District, Perth was given a courthouse and jail. Opened in 1821, the building was two storeys high, with the courtroom on the second floor and five cells on the main floor, along with the jailer's two-room apartment. According to contemporary accounts, its cells were routinely filled with brawling Irish loggers from the Ottawa River. The building was declared inadequate, and, following a fire in 1841, construction on a new courthouse began, with

The Lanark County jail in Perth reflects the stunning architectural heritage of this eastern Ontario heritage town.

jail facilities to be in the rear portion of the building. These, however, also proved to be inadequate, and, twenty years later, a new jail was completed and a new registry office soon after that.

Designed by H.H. Horsey of Ottawa, the two-storey stone structure contained 18 cells in four wards, with separate exercise yards for male and female inmates. The front portion of the structure housed the jail's governor until the 1950s. The first provincial inspection report in 1862 counted 27 inmates, including a surprising number of women, 16 in all. Charges ranged from murder and assault, to vagrancy and concealing the birth of a child. In addition, six inmates were diagnosed as being insane. The most common offence was found to be "breach of indentureship by leaving one's master,"[46] a charge which would be unheard of today. In 1873, a further inspection revealed that of the eight male prisoners, one couldn't move, another was blind and helpless, a third was paralyzed, and a fourth "ruptured." None, the report complained, should be in a jail.

In 1851, one Francis Beare, who had been convicted of killing William Barry, was hanged. His defense was that his wife had made him do it. On May 23, before a crowd assembled in front of the courthouse, he plunged to his death. Unable to find an executioner locally, the sheriff had to resort to hiring a prisoner from the penitentiary in Kingston to perform the deed in exchange for freedom. Following the hanging, rumours swirled that the crowd was anxious to lynch the hangman who was spirited away to Smiths Falls by stagecoach.

While five executions were carried out, including one for the mutilation of a cow, few inmates in the Perth jail were there for criminal acts. Most were housed there for shelter, having been committed under the Vagrancy Act. Many of these were "tramps" from the railway towns of Carleton Place and Smiths Falls. In fact, November was known in the jail as "tramp season" in Perth. With the completion of a proper house of refuge in 1903, the pressure on jailing the homeless eased.

Local newspapers often carried accounts of county crimes. A "most daring robbery was perpetrated in Pakenham," quoted one story. One "Mr. Otterson was attacked on the street by four raftsmen who cut off the skirt of his coat in the pocket of which they expected to find money...We are glad to hear that the parties are known, and steps are being taken to bring them to justice."[47] In another case, some loggers had been on a "spree at the house of a Frenchman. Two of the men revisited the place and were refused admission whereupon the door was kicked. The tenant discharged a gun through the aperture and struck one of the men in the forearm. The man who did the shooting has left for parts unknown."[48]

The jail's facade has been altered over the years, with a porch being removed and a new entrance created at the ground level. The governor's residence was converted to accommodate offices. Then, on October 4, 1994, the province closed the jail. Much of the interior remains in its original condition with its narrow corridors, tiny cells, one metre by two-and-a-half metres, and the unused gallows.

The building can be found at the corner of Beckwith and Craig streets, a short distance south and east of the town's historic main street and scenic turning basin. The courthouse stands immediately to the west of the jail.

## PETERBOROUGH

The City of Peterborough is a scenic place, with historic homes and institutions situated on its rolling hills. Near the centre of town, and covering one such hill high above the Otonabee River, stand Peterborough's county courthouse and its former jail. Like most in Ontario, they have seen their share of controversial trials and morbid executions.

The first execution was that of William Brenton in 1873 for the murder of Jane Payne and her young cousin. His defense of insanity found no takers and he was led off to the gallows. An autopsy following his death showed that his brain was badly misshapen; he had indeed been insane. One of the strangest trials was that of an English teenager named Robert Henderson. He had arrived in Canada in 1909 from a crime-ridden life in West Hartlepool, England. To make ends meet he wandered the countryside doing odd jobs. At the home of the MacPherson sisters near Norwood, he offered to cut firewood for them, but they declined. In retaliation he struck one of the women with an axe and fled. A neighbour saw the attack and gave chase until Henderson surrendered to Constable Fred Barrett of Havelock, where he was placed in the lock-up. Doctors testifying at this trail confirmed he was a "high grade imbecile" but would nonetheless remain a constant danger to society. Found guilty, Henderson was hanged on June 23, 1910.

The next executions occurred a decade later when two Austrian immigrants, Michael Bahri and Tom Konek, led three others on a raid of a gang of quarry workers near Havelock. But when Konek stumbled on some stairs, his gun discharged and killed one of the workers. After fleeing with $800, they were quickly caught and charged with murder. The ringleaders, Konek and Bahri, were sentenced to hang while the others spent the rest of their lives in the dungeon-like confines of Kingston Penitentiary. To further add to their agony, on their way to the gallows the doomed men were forced to march past their prepared graves.

Peterborough's last hanging, which took place in 1933, was that of the personable Edward "Stonewall" Jackson. He had arrived from Milwaukee with his partner Eugene Lee, intent on buying a farm together. However, Jackson found out that Lee had cheated him on the purchase and, following a heated argument, shot him. Despite testimony that the killing might have been self-defense, Jackson was sentenced to death. While in jail, he became friendly with the jailer and staff, and shook each of their hands while he went to the gallows.

Of the five men executed, four were buried in the jail yard where they remained until their bodies were rediscovered and disinterred in 1994. Despite additions over the years, the tiny one-man cells remained

The entrance to the Peterborough County jail lies behind the courthouse.

in use until the end, although none of the earlier inmates could have imagined the telephones and TVs which modern prisoners would use.

The jail was built in 1842, two years after the courthouse. Stone for the building was brought in from a quarry where Jackson Park, in the north end of Peterborough, is located today. In 1863, the jail was considerably altered, with accommodations for the jailer and turnkey (the keeper of the keys), being added. Three generations of the same family held the job of sheriff, beginning with James Hall in 1856, his son James Albro Hall following in 1872, and J.A.'s son in turn in 1923. The family dynasty lasted until 1936.

The courthouse, now a full county building, looks out over Victoria Park in central Peterborough from its perch high above the Otonabee River. It is located on the east side of Water Street between Murray and Brock streets. The jail entrance lies immediately behind the courthouse. The jail was closed in 2002 and in 2003 renovations began, which continue to this day.

## SIMCOE

Although he was hired in 1975 to tear down Simcoe's historic jail, Carlos Ventin instead turned out to be its saviour.

At first, the courthouse and jail for the District of London lay in the now long-forgotten village of Charlotteville, located near Turkey Point on Lake Erie. In 1813, the functions were moved further inland to Tisdale's Mills, and placed in a brick building. Shortly afterwards, the name of the town was changed to Vittoria. Following their destruction by fire in 1825, the court and jail were moved to the more populous and growing Town of London. Anxious to have these functions returned to their town, the residents of Vittoria petitioned to have the district separated, with their town once again being designated as the district seat.

When the partition, which created the District of Norfolk, finally did occur in 1837, the district seat went instead to Simcoe whose petition had more names. The angered Vittorians argued that the Simcoe petition contained the ineligible names of dozens of children, but to no avail. To satisfy the legal requirements for a district seat, Simcoe hurriedly erected a two-storey wooden structure to house both court and jail. However, an 1842 government inspection of the facility spared no words in criticizing the jail—referring to it as "a careless and dishonest state of erection,"[49] with locks that were "entirely useless," and cells which could not be ventilated. In 1846, Toronto architect William Thomas was hired to plan a new jail. A two-storey brick governor's residence was built on the front, with the cell blocks attached behind. Two years later the cells were ready.

Some of the stories of the inmates reflect the social conditions that dominated the times. In 1863, one boy was reported to have been going to school from the jail as his mother had died in captivity. Another boy had been imprisoned for four years without having been sentenced for anything. The inspector of jails noted that "although dictated no doubt by benevolent motives, (these are) highly irregular

The Norfolk County jail in Simcoe was one of the first to be rescued by architect
Carlos Ventin.

and an entire misappropriation of the prison."[50] In fact, few of the
inmates were placed there on serious charges. The inspector's report
of 1893 lists convictions for such crimes as watering down milk, allowing hogs and cattle to run at large and shooting on a Sunday, as well as
the more usual drinking violations.

However, the most stunning charges came in 1908 when the chief
of police, Archibald Malone, was himself locked up, charged with
attempting to kill his constable, William Wilkins. While investigating
suspicious late night activity in the town's park, Malone shot Wilkins
several times in the back, leaving him for dead. Badly wounded,
Wilkins managed to crawl to the local doctor's office where he recovered sufficiently to testify against his chief. As the trial unfolded, it was
revealed that both men had long been involved in a string of unsolved
burglaries. The jury took just two hours to convict Malone and sentence him to life in Kingston Penitentiary. Wilkins, however, was let
off with time served. While Wilkins returned to England, Malone was
released to enlist in the First World War.

The last hanging took place in 1953 when Emerson Shelly was executed for the murder of Christian Shoup. Shelly was buried, ironically, in Charlotteville, the site of the first district courthouse and jail.

By 1975 the jail had served its purpose and was scheduled for demolition. The job was assigned to architect Carlos Ventin. However,

believing that the historic building could be recycled for less cost, Ventin convinced the county council to change its mind and began the transformation. Today, while the exterior retains its original appearance, the interior has been totally revamped and expanded, and now houses the town's main library.

Built in an Italianate style of red brick, the jail is one of Simcoe's few pre-1850 buildings to survive. In fact, the entire county complex, including the former jail, courthouse and registry office, is considered to be a grouping of buildings unrivalled among Ontario's municipal heritage buildings. The three buildings encircle a small park at the west end of Peel Street two blocks west of Norfolk Street, the town's main thoroughfare.

## STRATFORD

Were it not for its world famous Shakespearean Festival, Stratford would offer little to entice visitors. Certainly not its climate, for it is southern Ontario's wettest community; certainly not the scenery for the area immediately around it is numbingly flat, and certainly not its architecture, for most of its homes are modest and its stores, with a few exceptions, ordinary. These characteristics reflect Stratford's lesser-known role as having formerly been one of Ontario's most important railway towns.

Several of its buildings stand out from the rest. The railway station, a grand brick building, now underutilized by a mere four trains a day, the massive city hall plunked in the middle of a triangle of plain commercial buildings, and the county building, a towered structure embellished with a patternwork of two-tone bricks.

And then there is the jail. Built separately from the courthouse in 1886, its architect, George Durand, gave it a very domestic feel. Facing the street is the yellow brick governor's house, which looks as though it belongs in the residential part of town, while the yard and cell blocks are attached behind. The first jail, however, was decidedly less pleasant for all concerned. Situated within the original courthouse, both were built in 1853 to allow Perth to become a full county, with Stratford as the county seat. And at the time, Stratford needed something to bolster its image.

The first building to be erected here on the banks of what was then called the Little Thames River was the Shakespeare Tavern. Located halfway between Guelph and Goderich, it became a stopping place for stagecoaches travelling on the Huron Road. Although the site had been

Stratford's architecturally striking Perth County jail, still in use, pales next to the popularity of the town's Shakespearean Festival.

laid out by William "Tiger" Dunlop[51] in 1832, as part of his scheme to develop the vast expanse of land known as the Huron Tract, Stratford remained a cluster of huts around a pair of mills until 1850. In that year the County of Perth was created and Stratford became the county seat. With the arrival of the politicians, the judges and the bureaucrats as part of its new status, the dismal little place finally began to grow.

One early plan for the jail was rejected because it would have located the cells beneath the courtroom. A draft of air from the cells might have been the means "of carrying infectious effluvia into the courtroom," it was reasoned.[52] Finally, a two-storey block of 12 cells on each storey was built. Robert Kay was appointed as the head "gaoler" with 51 constables working under him. His position which paid him 80 pounds a year. Among his duties were doing "the washing for the prisoners (not the debtors) and scrubbing the gaol."[53] The surgeon for the jail, with the interesting name of Dr. Hyde, was paid 12 pounds per year.

However, the new courthouse and jail quickly proved to be inadequate. In 1869, the provincial inspector's report complained that the "lower cells were fit only for dark punishment cells... and the windows were mere portholes, unfit for either light or ventilation."[54] In 1871, the inspector further discovered to his disgust that a girl only seven years old had been committed as "a vagrant and loose person...which I learned really meant she had been abandoned by her parents...gaol was not a proper place for her."[55] The *Perth County*

*Historical Atlas* further complained, "The courthouse and the jail... fail to give satisfaction or accommodation to the many increasing requirements of the public and the county officials."[56] Little action, however, was taken to replace either the jail or the courthouse, which too had come under equally scathing criticism.

In 1868, the province suggested Stratford as a possible location for one of three provincial prisons. But no action was taken to relieve the unbearable conditions that confronted the users of the court and the inmates of the jail. Finally, in 1884, an inspection by Dr. O'Reilly, the provincial prison inspector, and Kivas Tully, the provincial architect, concluded that the jail was "utterly unsuited on sanitary grounds."[57] In 1886, new buildings were started in a more central location, and a year later were open for business.

Today, the spectacular courthouse dominates the main street from its perch high on a rise of land, overlooking the Avon River. Built from mauve-coloured Credit Valley sandstone and yellow brick, it is described as an architectural mix of Italianate, Romanesque and Queen Anne styles. Rounded windows stretch two storeys into the prominent gable, while a slender tower stretches skyward beside the main section.

The jail witnessed only three executions over its lifetime, the last coming in 1954 when a soldier named Reuben Norman was hanged for the murder of his 17-year-old girl friend. The most shocking execution was that in 1895 of an itinerant named Almede Chattelle for the gruesome murder and mutilation of a 13-year-old girl near Listowel, a small farming community 45 kilometres north of Stratford. Because the details were similar to those attributed to the elusive Jack the Ripper, local officials contacted the investigators in England to determine if Chattelle might even be the Ripper himself. So outraged were the local citizens by the offence, described in morbid detail by two local newspapers, that rumours of a lynch mob began to swirl. When Chattelle was finally executed, nearly six months after the murder, more than 50 invited spectators crowded into the prison yard to witness the event, even though public hangings had been banned by that time.

The jail fronts onto St. Andrews Street, around the corner from the looming courthouse, while between the two sits the smaller, but equally elegant, registry office. Today both courthouse and jail retain their original roles, while the registry office has taken on the task of housing the county archives.

## WALKERTON

Like many of the towns and villages in Ontario's western farm belt, Walkerton has not gone out of its way to become a tourist destination. Despite its pleasant situation on the banks of the Saugeen River, and its revitalized main street, there is little here to attract the tourist's eye. And the heritage jail and courthouse reflect that ambivalence. Despite their history and their architectural qualities, both the jail and courthouse have been altered in such a way as to diminish those features.

Perhaps this muted approach to its historic jail is because Walkerton should not have been the county seat in the first place. When the County of Bruce was created in 1860, the local reeves submitted no fewer than ten candidate communities for the cherished role, a few of which no longer even exist. To resolve the squabble, the provisional county council opted to call for a vote by Bruce County residents to choose their capital. When the final count came, Walkerton placed third, behind both Paisley and Kincardine. For reasons never made clear, the provisional council disregarded the results and chose Walkerton.

Bruce County jail, located in Walkerton, was the site of a "fixed" execution.

In 1866, an Italianate courthouse, with a cupola atop an octagon, was built. Ultimately, the jail was positioned beside it. While council dithered over the jail's location, a temporary lock-up was placed in the basement of a house on the south side of town. There, the jail consisted of a single cell in the basement of the house, while the jailer's office and quarters occupied the main floor and second floor. This building stood until 1992 when it was demolished for a car dealership.

While a number of hangings occurred throughout the history of the jail, the last being during the Second World War, perhaps the most bizarre was that of the man who didn't die. In 1868, John Hoag was sentenced to death for murder. On the day scheduled for the execution, the hangman slipped the rope around Hoag's neck. As the trap door swung open he plunged to the end of the rope, and the doctor proclaimed him dead; a few days later his coffin was lowered into a grave. But the judge who had sentenced him, while visiting the United States some weeks later, was startled to see, alive and walking the streets, the very man he had ordered hanged. When the facts came out, it was revealed that a double rope had been attached to him, the real rope being secured to a hook hidden under his clothes, instead of around his neck where a fake noose was placed. Both hangman and doctor were involved in the scam, a deceit which even made its way into *Ripley's Believe It or Not*.[58]

Many of the stories around the jail's inmates have a decidedly "wild west" air about them. The Campbell Gang, which lived in the then dense forests north of Walkerton, had only disdain for the law. In one infamous episode they captured the sheriff who had gone to arrest them and forced him to eat his arrest warrant. Finally, a posse caught up with the fugitives near Kincardine and trapped seven of them in a farmhouse. The standoff lasted until the sheriff set fire to the house. The Campbells stormed out with their guns blazing. Two were shot and captured. Their leader, Colin Campbell, was sentenced to prison. The rest escaped and fled to Manitoulin Island where they bought a property that had previously belonged to Joseph Walker, the town's founder. Incredibly, the survivors sued the police but lost their case. An execution scheduled in 1962 did not take place as capital punishment was nearing its final days in Canada, even though the gallows had been built and the hangman was waiting in town.

One of the largest features of Bruce County is the vast Greenock Swamp, found about 15 kilometres west of Walkerton, dark and dense and filled with quicksand. During the prohibition era, however, it became a hotbed of stills making illegal whisky. As the swamp was nearly impenetrable, few moonshiners were ever apprehended. Even today some of old copper kettles used for making the moonshine still occasionally turn up in the swamp.

Despite the long and colourful history of the old Walkerton jail, there is little physically to celebrate that heritage. A large part of the facility was removed to make way for more parking, while much of the courthouse's Italianate facade was covered over with a newer addition in the 1950s. While the remaining wall of the jail yard is visible beside the parking lot, the entrance is harder to see, tucked into a narrow walkway behind the courthouse. The jail remains in use at this writing.

Both structures sit on a rise of land in the residential part of town, on the east side of Jackson Street and two blocks south of the downtown core.

## WELLAND

The main street of Welland has lost much of its historic significance. Most buildings of heritage value have been demolished to make way for a dreary bus depot, uninspired office buildings or simply parking lots. But in the midst of this urban desolation stands one of the region's grandest buildings. Looming above the empty avenue is the courthouse for the former County of Welland, and, tacked onto the back portion, is the former jail.

In 1855, the canal-side village of Merricksville was chosen over rivals Fonthill, Cook's Mills and Port Robinson to be the county seat of the newly formed Welland County. The village was renamed Welland, and Ontario's most prolific institutional architect, Kivas Tully, was hired to design the building. The jail was built to accommodate 44 male and 12 female prisoners and extended three storeys in height. It was described in an inspection report of 1884 as being a "substantial stone structure possessing all the qualifications for the health and safety of its inmates."[59] That year the jail welcomed 245 guests as the county was "far from enjoying an Arcadian freedom from offences against law and order," according to one observer.[60] One freedom denied to inmates was their choice of literature, especially if it was too "choice" as one inspector discovered. "Inappropriate literature was observed in one of the corridors," he wrote," "Wild Oats" being anything but proper material for a prisoner in a gaol."[61]

The jail's first execution took place in 1859 before a large crowd of spectators. With hoards of onlookers crammed onto bleachers perched on top of nearby hotels, Henry Byers was hanged for the murder of a local farmer named Thomas Phillips. The strangest prisoner, however, was one William "Townsend" who had been charged with killing a police constable in Port Robinson. The year 1857 was long before photographs were in common use, and the suspect managed, using friends as "witnesses," to convince the jury that he was someone other than

The Welland County jail stands on the main street of this canal city.

Townsend. He was acquitted. Later, he was charged in Cayuga for an earlier murder, but once again walked free from a hung jury.

Welland's jail may also have witnessed an early version of today's modern terror threats. In 1900, two men disembarked from the Niagara, St. Catharines and Toronto train. With suitcases in their hands, they walked toward Lock 24 on the Welland Canal. Here they lit fuses on their suitcases and fled. But the explosions proved modest and caused little damage to the gates of the lock. Had the blast been what they had intended, the water crashing through the ruptured gate would have flooded the Thorold Valley and likely would have killed thousands in the torrent's path. The pair were quickly located at a hotel in Niagara Falls where, with their mastermind, they were arrested and locked up in the Welland jail. At the trial it was learned that all three were Fenian[62] sympathizers and had intended to unleash terror on the area. All were convicted and received life sentences.

The jail's last hanging took place on January 17, 1958, when Thomas Laplante was hanged for killing a customer in a drugstore that he had robbed. He had forced the customer to drive to an isolated location where he bludgeoned him with a hammer. Twenty years after the hanging, the jail was closed. In 1984, the courthouse was declared a heritage building and restored along with the old jail portion. Most of the interior was totally revamped, although much of the exterior was preserved. Today the grand building, with the jail clearly visible behind it, still serves as a court building.

The buildings can be found on Main Street, east of King Street, in downtown Welland. A short block to the west, the historic lift bridge over the now disused portion of the canal that gave the town its birth, still carries traffic.

## WOODSTOCK

Among all Ontario's jails, both small and large, the one in Woodstock stands out. It is distinctive not just for its elegant Italianate style, but for its restoration work and, not least, for its inmates.

Built in 1854, it stands on five acres of ground originally set aside by Ontario's first Lieutenant-Governor, John Graves Simcoe. Little growth occurred there before 1826, the year London was named as the district seat. In 1849, the County of Oxford was separated from the larger and earlier District of London. The first order of business was to construct the necessary county buildings—a courthouse, a registry office and a jail. The jail, built from local yellow brick, was designed in a grand Italianate style with Tuscan towers flanking the entrance, and

A carving of the first felon to be executed in the Oxford County jail in Woodstock, stares beside its entrance.

an octagonal central tower from which the cell blocks all radiated, allowing the guards to watch all corridors from the same spot.

The first of Woodstock's five executions was that of Thomas Cook. An alcoholic, he was condemned to death in 1862 for the beating death of his wife. Because of his excessive weight, when his body plunged through the trap door on the scaffold, it separated from his head, which was left to roll on the ground before a stunned crowd of gasping spectators. His likeness was subsequently carved in a death mask that stares out at people to this day from its perch beside the front entrance.

While three other inmates subsequently met their fate at the end of a rope, the most famous was the charismatic Reginald Birchall. Birchall was a colourful Englishman who, with his wife, had fraudulently posed as "Lord and Lady Somerset." The couple became one of Woodstock's most celebrated residents. At the time, no one knew his true identity, or that he was nearly bankrupt. Returning to England, Birchall placed tantalizing ads in local papers asking for partners to co-finance land deals in Canada. Two responded, Douglas Pelly and Fred Benwell, both of whom accompanied the Birchalls back to Canada. Shortly after his arrival in the area, Benwell was found murdered in a nearby swamp, just east of Woodstock, near Princeton, Ontario. Pelly then became suspicious of Birchall's threatening behaviour toward him and alerted the police. Birchall was arrested and on September 29, 1890, was convicted of the murder. However, the impact of his personality on the court spectators, the media, and even on his captors, was hypnotic.

During his stay, Birchall even penned an account of the jail, referring to the institution as "Castle Cameron" after the jail's governor, John Cameron. His observations, mocking though they were, also offered a prisoner's view of life in a Canadian county jail. They provided insight on meals which he called "pernicious luxuries" brought to the "guests" by the "butler of the institution." The cells "without being elaborately furnished are comfortable, with all the provision for an extensive toilet being limited." As for activities in the jail, "a strange idea prevails here that too much exercise had a deterrent effect upon the body; consequently the area is limited by four walls, built high enough to keep out the biting winds which howl around this pile of rock."[63]

For the six weeks while Birchall sat in the Woodstock jail awaiting his execution, his jailer, James Forbes, came to know him well. He admired his prisoner's composure and eloquence, and was even moved to tears during the "tender meetings" between the killer and his wife. Birchall, in turn, called Forbes "a true friend, tried and trusted comrade, and a credit to his country."[64] Even following Birchall's execution, Forbes continued to receive letters from the murderer's widow.

Woodstock's final execution was the rare hanging of a woman, Elizabeth Tilford. She was convicted of poisoning her husband, and for that crime was put to death in 1935. In 1977, the province closed the old jail,

The county jail in Woodstock is one of Ontario's most stunning architectural buildings.

while county council pondered its fate. Ignoring a grant of $325,000 to help preserve the historic jail, council voted instead to demolish it. A "Save the Jail" committee was quickly organized and convinced a grudging council to reverse its decision. With further grants from the province, the county hired the Argentine-born restoration architect Carlos Ventin, who had guided the conversion of the jail in Simcoe into a library, to redesign the building as a Board of Health office.

Woodstock is a community of magnificent heritage buildings. The courthouse (1890) and registry office complete the county complex, while the old town hall (1852) and market stand on a main street of 19th century buildings. To complement it all, those who arrive in Woodstock by VIA Rail, disembark at one of Ontario's oldest and most elegant small town train stations.

The jail stands on Buller Street opposite Victoria Park, two blocks east of Vansittart Street, "millionaire's row," and two blocks north of Dundas, the main street.

# THE LOCAL LOCK-UPS

**W**hile the county jails took care of the convicted felons, the local lock-ups typically housed the Saturday night drunks, vagabonds, and, on occasion, wandering livestock. Only those towns that were designated as the administrative centre of each county would contain a county jail; smaller towns and villages would more often contain a cell or two in the basement of the town hall. Where this was not possible, or where there was no town hall, as in the case of unincorporated villages (those communities that had not yet qualified for village status), then a separate facility with two or three cells, and possibly space enough for a constable's desk, would be built, usually down some lane or behind the main street.

## BEAVERTON

It is safe to say that the old stone jail in Beaverton has been around a lot. Not just in longevity but in location as well.

Beaverton began as a port on Lake Simcoe and mill site on the Beaver River. Growth progressed slowly though the 1830s and '40s. However, when legislation was passed in 1847 requiring all unincorporated villages to erect lock-ups, Beaverton was large enough for its own jail. Like most small jails, the building was situated close enough to the town hall so that prisoners didn't need to be transported too far, and yet far enough away from public thoroughfares to not be offensive to the law-abiding townspeople. The building was box-shaped, constructed of local stone, and contained three tiny cells. The doors were two-ply oak with only a fist-sized hole for communication. As with most

The Beaverton lock-up was relocated to the town's museum complex.

local lock-ups, the primary guests were local drunks and vagrants. However, in the early days, travellers who were down on their luck and couldn't afford a room in one of the five hotels were offered a bed of straw and a meal in the jailhouse before continuing on their way.

"The lock-up accommodated five tramps on Friday night last," noted the *Beaverton Express* of 1896. "All looked very respectable and pleaded scarcity of work as reason for necessity. They came from the north in hope of obtaining work on the Trent Valley Canal."[1] The paper also chastised Constable Scott for mixed priorities, ignoring crime while pursuing cows. "One evening last week a person who should be behind bars stood in the alleyway between Morrison and Westcott's stores making indecent exposure of his person. The constable should make it his business to bring the scoundrel to justice."[2] Then, in another piece, "Constable Scott seems determined that the town's cow bylaw should not be a dead letter in this village and on Saturday impounded several animals from wandering on the street."[3] Locals will also mention the story of the prisoner who escaped only to be cornered up a telegraph pole. The constable hastened the escapee's return by hurling eggs at the miscreant until he had enough, and chose to surrender.

In 1911, the old Beaverton Town Hall was closed and moved back from the road to make way for a new hardware store, while a new town hall was erected across the way. Because the new building contained more modern cells, the old jail was closed. For more than 80 years it was

The interior of the Beaverton lock-up has been restored to its jail days.

used variously as a garage, a storage area for the Boy Scouts' newspaper drives, a sports store and an art gallery. During this time alterations were made, and a commemorative plaque erected. Then, in 1994, the local branch of the TD bank purchased the old hardware store with the intention of demolishing it to allow for a larger banking facility. To make way for parking, the old jail would have to go as well. As part of its community involvement, the bank offered the building to the Beaverton Thorah Eldon Historical Society, giving them both funding and time to move it. After the old store had been levelled, Charles Matthews' Heavy Movers jacked up the jail and transported it a block west to its new home, the site of the town's Beaver River Museum complex, where the stonework restoration was carried out by Peter De Groot.

Still, more funding was still needed for both the move and the restoration, but no grants were available from the provincial government. The needed additional money came from the Foster Hewitt Foundation and Jackman Foundation, as well as from a popular authors' night hosted by Canadian author Timothy Finley, along with a variety of other local fundraisers. A number of local fundraising events were to follow.

Today, the old jail, located at the west end of the main street, is open for visitors once again. The cells have been restored, one with its original door (and "inmate"). A video, *Romancing the Stones*, available for sale there, recounts the jail's history and its move.

It was interesting to note that shortly after the much-heralded rescue of the Beaverton jail, the little century-old lock-up in the neighbouring village of Brechin was demolished. That hamlet is now deprived of what would have been its only heritage attraction.

## BERENS RIVER

Much is made over which town in Ontario has the smallest jail. Tweed long claimed that it held the crown, only to relinquish it some time later to the smaller jail at Creemore. However, in the end, that claim equally could have been made by Port Dalhousie and Coboconk. Yet, despite all the rivalry, each must yield to the tiny single cell lock-up, part of the remote Ontario ghost town of Berens River.

The town began in 1936 when Dewitt Smith laid a townsite for his gold mining operation. The place was remote, two hours by plane from the gold town of Red Lake, itself at the end of the road, yet the closest settlement to Berens River. But the deposits in the area appeared to be rich and no expense was spared to fly in the construction material. Within a few months, the town could claim two bunkhouses, a dining hall, office, executive quarters and the mine

Ontario's smallest jail is in the ghost town of Berens River, north of Red Lake.

buildings themselves. Eventually, a road was opened to the site, but not without a quarrel between the governments of Ontario and Manitoba over who would pay for the road, which lay largely in the latter jurisdiction. While Manitoba was reluctant to subsidize a road that led to a mine in Ontario, the other government balked at the notion of financing a road that lay mostly in another province.

Following a compromise, the new road for the mine came into being, and the town could now be expanded. In 1941, Berens River added a school, apartments, a bowling alley, a swimming pool, several private dwellings, a police station and a tiny single cell lock-up. The entire building measured little more than two metres by two metres with a sturdy door and a tiny window well above the ground. Even though liquor was illegal, as on any mining claim, miners are an industrious bunch, and drunkenness occasionally got out of hand. The jail cell was frequently in use.

At its peak the town could claim a population of 600. But, by 1948, the gold deposit was dwindling and the workforce was cut back. Shortly after, the mine was closed down altogether. With no other settlement nearby or any other opportunities for employment, the population left the area, and Berens River soon became a ghost town. While some buildings were dismantled and removed, most were left in place, leaving a nearly complete townsite with no people. And among the bungalows, the bunkhouses and the apartments that stand silent and windowless, still sits Ontario's tiniest jail. The silent mining camp lies on the north shore of South Trout Lake and is accessible today only by float plane.

## BRACEBRIDGE

Tourists, entering the pretty Muskoka town of Bracebridge via Santa's Village Road, are unlikely to believe that the little wooden garage beside the cemetery was Bracebridge's first, and is now its only surviving, jail.

By 1870 settlers were streaming into the newly opened Muskoka District along the rugged and twisting Muskoka Road. Bracebridge developed as a mill town around the considerable water power of the falls on the North Muskoka River. As the streets filled with rowdy lumbermen and travellers, the government built a small lock-up. Here intoxicated revellers would sober up while awaiting their onward journey. The first constable was known as a "night watchman," and was equipped only with a pair of handcuffs and a cap bearing the words "Police."

The first lock-up in Bracebridge is still around even though all the town's subsequent jails have been demolished.

The lock-up was used until 1879 when it was replaced with a sturdier stone structure situated a short distance away. The wooden building was moved away, and a district courthouse built on the site. While the "Stone Cottage," as its replacement was lovingly referred to locally, continued to accommodate overnight guests, a larger district jail was added to the courthouse.

The "Stone Cottage," located in a lane behind the main street, was demolished to make way for additional parking spaces for a local office and the jail portion of the courthouse replaced with municipal offices. Yet, ironically, the first lock-up has managed to endure. Although much changed, it still retains one of its original cell doors. The lock-up, now in private hands and used only for storage, is known to the local people.

## BRUCE MINES

A generally non-descript row of restaurants and motels lining Highway 17 between Sault Ste. Marie and Blind River may look unexceptional to a traveller. But the Town of Bruce Mines is one of the oldest and most historic communities along the north shore of Lake Huron. Most of its heritage features, though, lie away from the highway. Among them is the old wooden jailhouse.

In 1847, Bruce Mines became the site of Canada's first copper mine, sending a shipment of copper ore by schooner to Boston. The settlement was named after James Bruce, the then Governor General of Canada. The village and first mine, worked and inhabited largely by Cornish miners,[4] appeared east of the current town centre. At the time it was little more than a shack town.

By the 1850s, Bruce Mines had been surveyed into a townsite and an application submitted to the government requesting designation as the district seat of Algoma. That application, however, was refused. Still, by the 1860s, Bruce Mines had boomed into a bustling mining town. Since the site lacked a jail, felons were housed in the local taverns before they could be transported to Sault Ste. Marie. Townspeople began to tire of the drunken and profane inmates and, in 1872, the sheriff of Sault Ste. Marie pleaded with Ontario's Attorney General, A. Crooks, to build a jail in Bruce Mines. However, when the mines closed soon after, the need for a lock-up dwindled and the plan was shelved.

Finally, in 1887, following the reopening of some of the mines, a small jail was constructed at the east end of the village. Four cells were installed, one in each corner, while the centre portion served as the jailer's office. With the arrival of municipal government in 1891, cells were added to the town hall, and the jail was closed. It had housed only one inmate over that period. During the Depression, itinerant vagrants desperate for work sought shelter in the old jail building, but soon after that period its days of incarceration were finished. Since then it has served as a meeting hall for Girl Guides and Boy Scouts. Following the Second World War, when the local school burned down, the jail was converted into a temporary school. The cells were removed, and heating and electricity installed. The bars, however, were left in place.

When Highway 17 was built through Bruce Mines, the lock-up was moved back to allow for the new roadway. Today it sits weathered and unused, hidden by a growth of trees. Still, it

Bruce Mines's first lock-up has served, most recently, as a school.

remains a local heritage landmark. Along with the wooden Presbyterian church, which contains the museum, and the former Simpson Mine, which offers tours of its reconstructed buildings and original mine shaft, the little lock-up helps to celebrate the legacy of one of Ontario's most historic mining towns.

Bruce Mines lies about 90 kilometres east of Sault Ste. Marie on Highway 17.

## CAPE CROKER

Located on a remote peninsula north of Wiarton, the village of Cape Croker has been home to a small population of 600 Ojibway First Nation since 1858, when they were "convinced" to abandon their claims to the Owen Sound area. Prior to that the Saugeen Ojibway, or Chippewas of Nawash as they are more correctly called, had possessed a half million acres of land on the Saugeen Peninsula, known today as the Bruce Peninsula.[5] However the pressure for lumbering and settlement prompted the government to co-coerce the Native Peoples to relinquish their homes, their barns and their lands around Owen Sound and move to 6,000 acres of sand and rock at Cape Croker. Deprived of fertile soils in which to grow their crops, they nearly starved.

Nevertheless, the band struggled to survive on fishing and farming and their village developed along the shores of the wide sandy bay.

The little lock-up at Cape Croker is overwhelmed by its newer addition.

Although many modern homes, a new school and band offices can be found here, a number of older buildings still recount the early history of the community. Overlooking the waters of Georgian Bay are the historic agent's house, a pair of early churches, including the 1892 United Church, and the little stone single-cell jail. Dating from the 1880s, the jail has no surviving record of who was incarcerated or how long the structure served its role. Suffice it to say, it would have housed the usual drunks and rowdies overnight until they calmed down.

As southern Ontario's smallest jail, it measured a mere 2.5 metres by 4 metres with but a single door in front. Sadly, in recent years, a large storage shed was added to two sides, making the historic little structure difficult to distinguish as a one-time lock-up.

Cape Croker lies 15 kilometres northeast of Wiarton, and is east of Highway 6. Directional signs point the way.

## COBOCONK

In the battle for top honours as to which community can boast of having Ontario's smallest jail, Coboconk on Highway 35, about a half hour's drive north of Lindsay, is right in contention. Known simply as the "Old Coby Jail," it measures a mere 5 metres by 6.5 metres, and occupies a lot only marginally larger. The stone for the thick walls came from a nearby quarry. Two tiny cells were constructed along the rear portion, with the jailer's office at the front. The only light which could enter the windowless cells was through a small opening in the heavy wooden doors.

In 1899, Joseph Wakelin was appointed constable and locked people up for such offences as speeding with their buggies on the main street, or fishing on Sundays. But the most common offences were the usual drunk and disorderly and the charges for moonshining.

Despite the solid construction of the lock-up, not everyone stayed put, at least according to local lore. One such legend is that of a muscular man named Jack Bain who was reputed to be so strong that whenever he wanted to get out of jail, he would simply bend the bars. In another case of mysterious escape, the constable had locked up a man called Lee and went home. When he returned some time later, he found his prisoner sitting calmly outside the jail. When he investigated, Wakelin found to his amazement that the door was still locked and undamaged. How Lee exited from his cell and front door remains a mystery to this day.

The "Coby" jail in Coboconk was rescued by the town's senior citizens.

When Constable Wakelin retired in 1922, he was not replaced and the jail sat vacant for 50 years. Fearing the historic little lock-up might be torn down, am enterprising local seniors' group acquired it, sought funding, removed the cells and converted it to a summer gift shop for locally-made crafts.

Straddling the banks of the Trent Canal, Coboconk has long been a popular destination for cottagers, boaters and drivers following the scenic winding Highway 35. Other historic structures in town include the lime kilns on the south side of the canal, the former Nipissing Railway station, now relocated to a nearby park, and the Pattie Hotel, which dates to stagecoach days and which once provided many of the inebriated inhabitants of the little Coby jail.

The Coby jail lies on Water Street a few steps west from Highway 35 in the heart of the village.

## CREEMORE

For many years, residents in Tweed boasted of having "North America's smallest jail." That was until Reg Westbrooke, publisher of the *Creemore Star* and president of the Lions' Club challenged that claim. Measuring tape in hand, Westbrooke marched down to his community's old jail and

*Right*, Creemore's lock-up contends that
it is North America's smallest jail;
*below*, the interior has been preserved
as a jail and is open to visitors.

discovered, to his delight, that the Creemore lock-up was a foot smaller
than Tweed's. Tweed was about to be dethroned.

Creemore dates from 1843 when the first settler arrived on the
scene some 35 kilometres north of the present-day Creemore. Later, in
1873, the Hamilton and Northwestern Railway built a station by the
main street, and Creemore boomed into a bustling industrial village.

In 1892, the jail was constructed as part of a jail-building program ini-
tiated by the County of Simcoe, one that saw similar lock-ups built in
nearly a dozen county villages including Beeton, Hillsdale and Tottenham.

The cost for the structure came in at $425.25. While for the most part the jail housed only drunks and vagrants, its first inhabitant was not even human. As the *Creemore Star* noted, "The first prisoner to be introduced to our brand new lock-up was a female that spent a night there last week. The only charge against her (was that) she was as black as midnight, but as she very justly did not consider that was sufficient reason why she should be deprived of her freedom, she made a determined resistance against being incarcerated. She was finally landed however and when once there was as docile as any other cow."[6] While no other animals came to call the jail home, the cells did welcome a variety of guests until the 1940s, when the jail was closed.

According to Chris Raible of Creemore, it appears that this jail was a so-called "police jail" that served as a holding tank. Prisoners were held there until they could be put on a train to Alliston and be incarcerated there.[7]

The 5 metre by 6.5 metre building is constructed of local limestone. Three tiny windowless cells line the wall to the right of the entrance, with little room left over for the jail office. Situated behind the library, a block east of the main street, the jail is open to visitors during the summer and a sign now proclaims it as the continent's smallest jail. Walking tours of the popular village also lead past a variety of heritage homes, churches and stores, many of which now cater to the day tripper. Restaurants, gift shops, a local bookstore and the Creemore brewery all add to the appeal of this attractive little country town.

Creemore lies on Simcoe County Road 9, between County Roads 124 and 42 and just off the Airport Road, north of the Dufferin County Museum and Archives.

## HILLSDALE

Hillsdale is one of those too frequently overlooked places that lie in rural Ontario. A blink of the eye and you would pass it. With a main street which consists of little more than a gas station and a pair of stores, it seems to be too small to have once warranted a jail of its own. Yet, just down a short side street on the west side of historic Highway 93, there it sits. The village dates from the opening of the Penetanguishene Road in 1812. This route was laid out to allow the passage of troops and arms to the naval station at Penetanguishene during the

The historic Hillsdale jail is found along the historic Penetanguishene Road.

War of 1812–14. More than 70 taverns were said to have once lined the route, and Hillsdale became a busy stopover for stagecoaches and military convoys.

Following the Ontario Order-in-Council in 1847, which required the construction of lock-ups in small villages, Simcoe County built its first jail in Orillia in 1852. Seven others quickly followed in Bradford, Collingwood, Penetanguishene, Orangeville, Coldwater, Stayner and Rosemont. By 1894, more lock-ups had been approved for Cookstown, Beeton, Creemore, Tottenham, Elmvale, Washago and Wyebridge.

In 1900, the county granted the Township of Medonte $400 to build a jail in the village of Hillsdale, to control the rowdies who routinely tumbled from the taverns. In return, the township was responsible for the pay of the caretaker, the supply of firewood, and a per diem for a constable. According to the county bylaw, the jail had to be a minimum of 5 metres by 6.5 metres (about 15 feet by 20 feet), 3.3 metres (10 feet) high with walls at least half a metre (18 inches) thick and constructed of brick or stone. Floors had to be of concrete or stone and the doors of oak six centimetres (two inches) thick. The three cells had to have iron doors, "suitably fastened."

In 1906, the local newspaper noted that a "full gang is laying eight thousand feet of sidewalk and their new lock-up is about completed. Work speaks louder than words."[8] When finished, the jail, built of a mix of stone and brick, measured 6.5 metres by 9 metres. The exterior was covered with plaster and the roof with metal sheeting. The cells lined up along the rear of the building with an ample office area in front. Each individual cell measured three metres by two metres or twice the width of many county jail cells, each with a small window and full iron door. The interior ceiling was pressed metal with a diamond and floral pattern.

As few records were kept on local jails, little is known about many of its inhabitants, except they would have been the predictable mix of drunks and vagrants. In 1912, one miscreant was fined $1 for riding a bicycle on a sidewalk (a time-honoured problem it would seem). In 1931, the records show that $4.75 was paid for the housing and feeding of a tramp, a common occurrence during the Depression Years.

From about the 1920s its uses were expanded to include council meetings, polling stations and storage. Today, little has changed inside. The cells remain in place, while chairs, a desk, a wood-burning stove, benches and a sign saying "The Court House" recount its various functions. Although largely unused, it has been designated as a local heritage structure and honoured with a heritage plaque. Heritage lingers across the road as well in the form of the now abandoned Hillsdale hotel, a survivor from the lusty days of stage travel.

Hillsdale lies on Highway 93 about eight kilometres north of the busy Highway 400.

## LITTLE CURRENT

It is a testimony to its sturdy construction that the little stone jail in Little Current, on Manitoulin Island, has outlived every other building in the village. Situated on Lake Huron's scenic North Channel, which separates Manitoulin Island from the mainland, Little Current began as a port for vessels plying the waters of Lake Huron. When the Algoma Eastern Railway built a massive swing bridge to the island in the 1880s, Little Current boomed. Its main street developed along the shoreline, while homes and churches were built up the hill from the water.

Among them stood the little jail, built in 1878. It was one of many designed by the Ontario Department of Public Works under the supervision of Kivas Tully who was responsible for many of Ontario's public buildings. (Victoria Hall in Cobourg and the courthouse and jail in Gore Bay are two examples.) One of the early jailers went by the

Little Current's lock-up is one the oldest buildings in the Manitoulin Island town.

name of Potts, while in 1910, the provincial constable responsible for the community was J. Ramesbottom. Since that time, many of the village buildings have been destroyed by fire, or replaced with more modern structures. But the jail has survived throughout.

Measuring six metres by nine metres, the jail is not Ontario's smallest, but it did contain just two cells. Most of the jail's occupants were of loggers and sailors who were caught celebrating their time off a bit too vigorously, or bootleggers making moonshine in the nearby woods. Not all were happy with their incarceration. In one case, a pair of Irishmen made good their escape by having one play a fiddle to mask the noise of the other sawing through the bars. Another fugitive, a local bootlegger, was not so lucky. His bones were found five years afterward just a short distance away. He had, it was concluded, escaped only to become lost in the woods.

The lock-up remained in use until 1952. From the 1930s until the time of its closure, it was used for a library, local council meetings and the OPP office and lock-up—all at the same time. Book borrowers would occasionally have to face the sulking inmates, some of whom might have been relatives. Finally, when both the OPP and the library found new facilities, the jail was closed for good. It now functions simply as storage space. Still, it is considered to be one of Little Current's heritage buildings, and perhaps its most genuine link with the past.

Little Current today is a boater's "mecca," providing dockage and shopping for modern-day sailors plying the tossing waters of the

North Channel. The lofty white peaks of the La Cloche Mountains provide a spectacular backdrop for the setting. Here, the only land link between the world's largest freshwater island, and the mainland, remains the old railway swing bridge.

Little Current lies on Highway 6 about 45 kilometres south of the Trans Canada Highway (Highway 17) and a like distance north of South Baymouth, the terminus of the ferry connecting Manitoulin to Tobermory.

## MADOC

Behind the lovely stone St. Peter's Presbyterian Church in Madoc stands a strange little stone building, one that many locals insist served as the town's earliest lock-up. Capped with a small cupola, it resembles neither barn nor cabin, but it does share one thing in common with Ontario's other small jails, its shape and dimensions. While most local historians believe it did originally serve as a jail, this has not been the case in living memory. Nor are there any written records of that use.

Madoc began as a mill village, deep in the hills of Hastings County. By 1855 it could count 40 buildings, including two flour mills. When the Hastings Colonization Road was surveyed to open the lands north of Madoc in the 1860s, the village became the jumping-off point for settlers headed for the free land grants along that bush trail. But it was the discovery of gold on the Richardson farm by Marcus Powell in 1866 that turned Madoc into a gold rush town.

The site of Ontario's first gold rush was actually at Eldorado, a dozen kilometres further north. But it was at Madoc where the prospectors outfitted themselves for the gold fields. Hotels and taverns were hastily built in both places turning the two villages into bustling boom towns. When many of the gold mining claims proved to be fraudulent, the miners threatened to riot. To keep control, a special unit of mounted police from Belleville was hastily assembled and sent to Madoc to set up a headquarters. They built a two-storey wooden barracks behind the Presbyterian church, and beside it added a stone building which many claim they intended to use as a jail. Their cost of construction in 1867 was $3000, more than enough for both buildings.

On April 27 the troops clattered into town, looking, according to the local newspaper, "like a troop of cavalry rather than a body of men intended to fulfill the civil functions of policemen. They wear a military uniform and carry swords of the right stamp to deal with the desperate classes who infest gold digging regions."[9] Their uniforms, according to the paper, were blue with gold buttons and facing, and caps, their main duty to patrol the streets of this now bustling little town. Although they were eagerly welcomed by the town's beleaguered residents, they were also accused being too zealous on at least one occasion. According to the *Madoc Mercury*, "...although the Mounties conducted themselves with moderation, the people saved them from excess zeal in their quest of Mr....for simply making a remark while they were taking a man to the lock-up for public profanity."[10] Things quickly quieted down in the gold fields, and the mounted police left.

In 1873, a new town hall was built with two cells in the basement, a standard arrangement for most town halls in 19th century Ontario. However, this little lock-up was so damp that few were left in it overnight. Nor was it particularly secure. When Constable Sills left one man in it to run an errand, the inmate slipped out of his cell and reached the constable's destination before Sills. By 1970, these cells had been removed and the town hall converted to community uses.

Madoc today bears no resemblance to its lusty days as a gold rush town. It is a quiet residential town with a small range of stores, churches

Debate still swirls as to whether or not this stone building in Madoc served as a lock-up during Ontario's first gold rush.

and homes, much like any other small town in Ontario. But what of the strange stone building behind the church? An inspection of the interior reveals no sign of cells or even of a ceiling. While the windows are small with wooden bars, consistent with lock-up windows, the building has no internal divisions.

The conclusion, then, is that it was likely built by the mounted police as it was beside their barracks. It clearly served no function relative to the church. Its dimensions and sturdy construction resemble those of a typical lock-up. Therefore, it was in all probability built for that purpose. But with the police stay being so brief, and the new town hall lock-up being in place very soon afterward, it may have seen few inmates, and then only over a very brief period of time. Still, there's nothing like a little mystery.

Madoc lies south of the intersection of Highways 7 and 62, about 40 kilometres north of Belleville.

## MANITOWANING

If any region can boast of its preserved lock-ups, it is Manitoulin Island. Found here are the remarkable Gore Bay Jail Museum, the little stone lock-up in Little Current, a renovated lock-up in Providence Bay and the jail house museum in Manitowaning.

Located on the east shore of the island, Manitowaning is one of Manitoulin's oldest settlements. It was located strategically on the island's first settlement road which linked the port of Michaels Bay (now a ghost town) with Little Current. Settlers arrived by stage or by steamer calling at the wharf. In 1883, J.T. Burns built a flour and gristmill on the waterfront, an operation which later became the Manitoulin Roller Mill. Then, in the 1930s, the tourists began to call, taking the car ferry *Norisle* or *Norgoma* from Tobermory on the north tip of the Bruce Peninsula. Originally, the ferry service ran to Providence Bay but later switched to using South Baymouth as its terminus.

As the town grew, and, as Manitoulin acquired district status, the community needed a lock-up. In April of 1878, the contract was awarded to the Law Building Company of Meaford on the condition that they finish the building by that October or face a steep penalty of $20 for each week which they were late. Five metres wide by roughly eight metres deep, the jail contained five cells, each equipped with an

The stone museum includes portions of the former lock-up. *Courtesy of the Assiginack Museum.*

iron bedstead and a bucket. The building was made of solid timber 30 centimetres square and covered with boards, all on a rubble stone foundation. A fence which measured 13 metres by 20 metres surrounded the structure. Built under the auspices of the provincial Department of Public Works, it was designed, as was that in Little Current, by provincial architect Kivas Tully. That portion of the interior not occupied by cells was for the jailer, but it soon proved to be too small, and, in 1883, a comfortable two-storey stone house was added to the front of the jail.

Throughout 1885, records show that only ten prisoners were held there, three charged with drunk and disorderly, two with giving liquor to Indians, and two for rape and assault. It would appear that only one inmate ever tried to escape, but made it no further than the day room. In 1945, the jailer's house became the municipal office and community library. Later, in 1955, the jail was converted into the Assiginack Museum and the cells removed. In 1976, the municipal office and library moved to new facilities, and the museum expanded into the stone house.

While the stone house stands intact, the exterior of the jail has become enclosed in additions and only the walls, one original window, a door that led to the day room and the fireplace remain from its days as a lock-up. However, in 1999, one of the cells was reconstructed to recount the building's original use. A log cabin and blacksmith shop have been added to the museum grounds. Across the road, beside the roller mill, sits the steamship *Norisle*, which operated from 1946 to 1974. Permanently docked, the ship now functions as a summer theatre. All of them form part of a heritage complex, here in one of Manitoulin's most historic towns.

Manitowaning lies on Highway 6, about halfway between Little Current and South Baymouth.

## NEWBURGH

Prior to the establishment of a province-wide police force, most of Ontario's towns and villages built local lock-ups of some description. Most were cells in the basement of a town hall; many others were small self-contained structures; a few, however, were placed in whatever was handy and sturdy.

Such was the case of Newburgh. Located on the Napanee River, the mill town of Newburgh was once, in area, the largest incorporated village in Canada West. But its five-and-a-half square mile town plot never filled in.

This building known as "The Barracks," on Newburgh's main street briefly served as a lock-up.

The townships located along the shoreline of Lake Ontario had been acquiring settlers since the arrival of the United Empire Loyalists in 1783. Following the establishment of Napanee at the point where the river entered the Bay of Quinte, people began to make their way along the banks of the river. One of them was David Perry who, in 1824, built a sawmill at a promising waterpower site where the water of the Napanee River tumbled over a ridge of rock.

The water power that lured Perry soon attracted other mills as well, and a thriving little mill village with the name Rogues Hollow sprang up, northeast of Napanee. For several decades the bustling mill town rivaled Napanee in growth, and an extensive street pattern covering five-and-a-half square miles was laid out. Hotels, stores, mills, homes and churches were built along them, many using the limestone which lay very close to the surface; others were made from the plentiful supply of local lumber. In 1850, Rogues Hollow lost its colourful name and was incorporated as a village with the name Newburgh.

Its rival, Napanee, however, was the first to attract a railway with the arrival of the Grand Trunk in 1857, and Newburgh, now a backwater, stagnated. Eighty-four of its buildings, most of them frame, were lost in a devastating fire in 1897, a disaster from which the village never fully recovered. Nor did the arrival of two railways, the Bay of Quinte line in 1884 and the Canadian Northern in 1912, do much to attract new growth. By this time Napanee had become the county seat, and Newburgh was forever destined to remain within the shadow of its one-time rival.

Among the many stone buildings that did survive the fire is a curious square-shaped two-storey stone building. Now a residence, it was built in the 1840s by R. Dowling. He made farm implements in the lower level while living on the upper level. Sometime between 1850 and 1872, the stone structure served as a jail and acquired the nickname it still clings to today—"The Barracks." As with most such lock-ups, it provided a cooling off period for the town drunks who frequented the local taverns.

In 1872, The Barracks was sold to a Mr. Mulholland, who opened a shoe factory in it. Today, it serves as a private home and is considered to be one of the village's oldest buildings.

Newburgh is a heritage treasure, well worth a visit. Despite the losses in the fire, the main street still contains a former blacksmith shop, a carding mill, a hotel and stores, all constructed of stone. A short distance off the main street is the original Bay of Quinte Railway station. The right of way was moved in 1912 when the Canadian Northern Railway laid its tracks through Newburgh and the old station has been a private home ever since.

Newburgh straddles the Napanee River beside County Road 1, some eleven kilometres northeast of Napanee.

## PORT DALHOUSIE

It was a close call, but the little jail in Port Dalhousie missed out by only a few centimetres from becoming officially Canada's smallest. There is no disputing, however, that among Ontario's "small jails," the one in Port Dalhousie is the oldest.

Built in 1845, close to Lock 1 on the Welland Canal, the jail was busy from the start. Not only did it have to cope with the local town drunks but also with the thirsty sailors, restless after a few too many days sailing the Great Lakes. Close by were the taverns and bars of Port Dalhousie's main street.

Inside the jail, the inmates were crammed into two small cells, each heated from the warmth of a small fireplace, which the inmates themselves had to stoke. The door was constructed of heavy iron, solidly fastened with framing bolts and latch, while the roof was clad in copper panels. The windows were framed in metal with vertical bars.

Port Dalhousie itself dates back to the construction of the first Welland Canal[11] in 1824, and was named in honour of George Ramsey, Earl of Dalhousie. The town grew as a place of lodging for the canal workers and the "tow-boys" who drove the horses that towed the schooners and barges through the canal's many wooden locks. In 1842, the government bought the canal, and began to replace the aging wooden locks with more solid stone structures. In 1875, a third even larger Welland Canal was built.

To relieve the pressure on the jail, which often was filled to overflowing, the local council passed a Tavern Law. The new law required that all taverns must provide furnished sitting rooms and at least four bedrooms. This was intended to give their inebriated customers a place to sober up rather than staggering out into the street and causing disturbances. Not only were the drunks routinely tossed

*Above*, Port Dalhousie's little lock-up is one of the continent's smallest as well as one of its oldest; *right*, the sturdy door on Port Dalhousie's lock-up once held inebriated sailors.

into the jail, but also those people who worked on Sunday. The town's mayor, Alex Muir, strictly enforced the local Lord's Day laws that prohibited any form of work or fun on Sundays. Prohibition in Ontario between 1916 and 1927 brought a new breed of inmates, those caught smuggling in beer on boats from Quebec.

Then, in 1932, yet another canal was built. Providing a new Lake Ontario entrance at Port Weller, five kilometres east, it bypassed Port Dalhousie altogether. The growth of the town came to a halt. The boats and the drunks moved on. And, with the arrival of the newly formed Ontario Provincial Police, the little jail was closed. But the community was determined to retain the heritage of the little lock-up, and, in 1979, it was designated as a heritage building. While some proposals would have moved it and converted it into a tourist information centre, it was instead left in place and became part of a restaurant and bar operation.

In 1989, the measuring tapes came out. While Tweed, which until then claimed to have the nation's smallest jail, measured at 4.9 metres by 6.1 metres; that in Coboconk proved smaller at 4.57 metres by 5.84 metres, but it in turn was edged out by that in Port Dalhousie which measured 4.6 metres by 5.8 metres. However, the smallest jail in southern Ontario to be officially measured turned out to be the one in Rodney measuring a mere 4.5 metres by 5.4 metres.

Today, Port Dalhousie has revived. It remains, as it has for years, a popular recreational destination in the summer with its lakeside park, its beach, and its historic five-cent carousel. But it is also a heritage treasure. Canal Street, the main street, still looking much as it did when the ships still called, overlooks the preserved stone lock from the second Welland Canal. The lock from the third canal is also preserved a short distance away. But the most curious of the village's historic features will always be one of Canada's smallest jails. Historic downtown Port Dalhousie can be found at the north end of Lakeport Road in St. Catharines.

Municipally, Port Dalhousie is now part of the City of St. Catharines. As the county town for Lincoln County, St. Catharines possessed the courthouse and county jail. Unlike in most county towns, the court and jail were not next to each other. The jail built in 1869 was a magnificent stone structure made of stone and Italianate in design. It was closed in 1973 when the Niagara Region Detention Centre was opened. After a proposal for a restaurant fell through, the city council, rather than preserve the building, allowed it to be demolished. This regrettable decision cost the city a key heritage attraction.

## PROVIDENCE BAY

Today, Providence Bay is a quiet lakeside community on the south shore of Manitoulin Island. Home to cottages, cabins and campgrounds, its sandy shore is washed by the lapping waves of Lake Huron. Although primarily a vacation playground, it still serves a year-round population of hardy "Haweaters," (the Islanders' local name for themselves), descendants of the early pioneers to this ruggedly beautiful land.[12]

In the beginning, times were tough. The long days and weeks in the bush felling trees for the lumber companies or for clearing land for farming had few rewards. What free time there was for the men usually consisted of boozing and brawling. To tame the rowdiest of the carousers, small lock-ups were built as overnight quarters. The smallest of Manitoulin's three little jails was that at Providence Bay.

While few of the miscreants were hardened criminals, or even memorable, one visitor does remain large in local lore. One day, sometime during the 1920s, an itinerant dentist arrived in town, residing in the local hotel (demolished in 2002). As permanent dentists could be found only in larger towns, he was a welcome visitor. One day, having sent off a patient's results to the nearest lab, he frequented the post office, anxious to receive the lab results. Drawn by the appeal of the local postmistress, one Fanny Ogle, his visits soon became more frequent. Then, following a prolonged binge in the hotel tavern, his visit

The Providence Bay lock-up now accommodates tourists to Manitoulin Island.

to the postmistress became more amorous than Fannie was prepared to accept. She complained to the local constable, Hardy Fulford, who marched the wayward dentist into the lock-up. Some members of the local citizenry thought it unseemly that a professional should be confined this way and took him home to sober him up. The good doctor quickly took the message and left behind his temporary home, and no doubt a few aching teeth.

A few years later, a large family was burned out of their home on the Government Road a short distance east of the village. The tragedy took the life of their infant baby. Shortly after, the father died leaving the family without support. To help out, the village agreed to house the family in the tiny jail, where the mother and her five remaining children had to endure the lack of heat in winter and water. By the late thirties the jail was closed as the Ontario Provincial Police came into force and incorporated cells into their own stations. For a number of years, a lone fisherman known simply as Skipper Les, resided there, the little jail's last permanent guest.

But today, it houses more visitors than ever before. Now renovated as a guest cabin, it has become part of Sullivan's Cottages, a resort popular with summer vacationers and fall hunters. The two cells have been replaced by a single bedroom, while the jailer's office is the living room and kitchen. One original door still rests on its hinges, while the exterior is now covered with stucco. A plaque which commemorates its 1912 construction sits prominently beside the front door.

Providence Bay is located on Highway 551, about 80 kilometres southwest of Little Current, and its former jail is a block west of the main street.

## RODNEY

With its dimensions of 4.5 metres by 5.4 metres, the little lock-up in Rodney is now considered to be southern Ontario's smallest jail, a full four centimetres shorter than that in Coboconk.

Rodney began as a farm service hamlet named Centreville, scarcely large enough for a jail. Then, in the 1870s with the arrival or a pair of railway lines, the Canada Southern and the Canada Air Line, the area around the two stations grew into a bustling commercial core. A new name was bestowed—Rodney, after the British Admiral of the same name.

The Rodney lock-up is claimed to be slightly smaller than its "smallest" rivals in Creemore and Port Dalhousie.

With the boom in hotels, and the coming and going of train crews and itinerant travellers, tipsy imbibers began to crowd the streets. The first village lock-up was a tiny room in the back of the old town hall, but it soon proved to be inadequate. In 1890, the township council authorized the allocation of $200 to build a separate facility. Situated at the southwest corner of the fairground, two blocks east of the main street, the yellow brick building contained two small cells, each measuring about two metres by three metres (5' 10" by 6' 9"). Neither had windows, although they did have full-length barred doors, while a pair of windows on the front of the building provided what little light there was. The floors were constructed of wood planking, while the cells had wooden walls and ceiling. The doors were made of solid steel bars, with the entrance to the lock-up being through a small door on the side of the building.

Constable Ludy patrolled the streets for many years, hauling the drunks off first to the local justice of the peace, and then to the little lock-up to sober up. The busiest times for the little jail were during the annual fall fairs. It is said that Ludy seldom locked the cell doors, allowing the occupants to leave on their own once they were sober.

A sign on Rodney's lock-up is part of the effort to preserve the building's heritage.

The building remained in use until the 1930s when a county police force was established, later to be replaced in turn by the Ontario Provincial Police. Since that time the little lock-up has served variously as a ticket office for the fairgrounds, a book exchange, and more recently as a summer tourist information centre. Indeed, highway signs now point the way to the building.

Little has changed inside. The walls remain unaltered, complete with inmates' carved messages. The cell doors still swing on their hinges, and the old pot-bellied stove still stands in the small office area. The only new addition is the historic plaque which celebrates the heritage of a long lost era.

Rodney is on Elgin County Road 103, a short distance south of Highway 401 and midway between London and Chatham.

## SILVER ISLET

Silver Islet was a town that lasted a mere decade. Its story, nonetheless, has filled a book or two, although that of its little log jail warrants but a footnote.

The geological feature known as Silver Islet is a skull-shaped shoal, which barely emerges from the grey waters of Lake Superior, a half kilometre from shore near the peninsula known as the Sleeping Giant. It would have remained simply another reef were it not for the presence, beneath the waves, of the richest silver vein ever discovered in Canada. Although prospectors knew of the deposit as early as 1842, their interest was not in silver, but copper. Until 1866, both silver and gold were reserved for the Crown, and private exploitation forbidden. When that restriction ended, the silver rush was on.

Miners wasted little time in sinking the first shaft in the winter of 1869–70, and the following October mining began as an open pit operation. It quickly became apparent that one of the first orders of business was to build a breakwater to hold back the lake's high waves. The first few wooden cribs were washed into the lake like so many match sticks. Finally, a solid concrete breakwater five metres high, and filled with 50,000 tonnes of rock, rose above the water. While the mine buildings and boarding houses were located on the islet itself, the town was built along the shore of the mainland sheltered by Burnt Island. By 1872 its population had reached 300.

The 52 workers' homes lined the shore road which was known as "The Avenue." The president's mansion and executive homes sat loftily at the eastern end around Sandy Beach. The place also contained two churches, a customs house, a general store, a bank and a jail. Situated away from the main part of the village, the jail was built behind the noisy stamp mill and contained five small cells that faced out onto a day room. The building also housed the jailer's office and apartment, and measured 7 metres by 9.5 metres. The first and only constable to live there was Thomas Gilmour.

Gilmour was kept busy rounding up drunks and rowdies. Although miners were only allowed one drink per shift to a maximum of three per day, both in the company bar and on the mainland, bootleg booze

The Silver Islet jail is now a cottage in this ghost town on Lake Superior's shore.

was easy to procure and heartily consumed. With miners of many different nationalities, fights, too, were common and were resolved with a cooling off period in the lock-up. Another crime, which the mine managers took more seriously, was the attempt to smuggle silver off the islet. Gilmour, the jailer, was given the thankless task of searching everyone as they left for the mainland.

While the mine produced record amounts of silver, the shafts, which stretched under the lake, leaked and needed constant pumping. The furnaces that powered the pumps were fuelled by coal, a commodity not found on the north shore, and had to be brought across the lake by boat. But, in 1883, the coal boat failed to show up. By March the supply was exhausted and the pumps fell silent.

In 1884, the miners trekked out and Silver Islet became a ghost town. But the scenic location, with its haunting buildings, was well known in the nearby cities of Port Arthur and Fort William, and, within a few years, regular excursion boats were carrying picnickers to the empty town. One visitor described the decrepit stamp mill as "tumbling down a little more each year, and the jail, its cell doors creaking eerily on massive hinges."[13]

By 1910 the townsite had become so popular that it was surveyed into lots and the buildings sold to summer vacationers. The jail, too, became a summer retreat, with additions made to the exterior, although the bars have remained on the windows. After visiting the ghost town in 1952, Beryl Scott wrote in the *Canadian Geographic Journal*, "Nearing the island we stopped at the little jail...good judgement had been used in choosing the site for this building whose chief duty was to cool off the over-indulgent. It was situated behind the main part of the village, its builders little dreaming that when a road was to be built down the peninsula, the jail would be the first relic of the old mine to receive visitors."[14] The landmark general store, left to weather for many years, was purchased by the late CBC broadcaster Lorne Saxburg[15] and given a new coat of blue paint. Today, the store is a key tourist attraction.

A provincial highway leads southward from the Trans Canada Highway to the preserved ghost town. Although the houses have been well kept, and are all privately owned, and a number of newer homes added, the permanent population stands at a mere eight people, just three more than could have been accommodated at the little log jail.

Silver Islet is located at the end of Highway 587, which leads south from Highway 17, roughly 70 kilometres east of Thunder Bay. The popular and scenic Sleeping Giant Provincial Park occupies most of the mainland peninsula.

## TWEED

For many years the townsfolk of Tweed boasted of having North America's "smallest" jail. And at 4.9 metres by 6.1 metres, the building appeared to have earned that title.

The little stone lock-up, however, was not Tweed's first. Until 1898, a pair of damp cells in the basement of the old town hall were used. When chronic flooding forced the village to come up with better facilities, a separate lock-up was built on the lot next door. The local paper described the inaugural inmate, "Lock-up Christened. The first inmate, Albert Smith, was arrested on a CPR caboose and charged with stealing a ride…he was later released when the conductor admitted that he allowed him in to keep warm."[16]

Being both a logging and railway town, Tweed suffered more than its share of drinking sprees. During the more festive occasions, the jail was known to have harboured as many as 16 inmates, all sleeping one off. During one street dance in 1938, when the three small cells were filled to overflowing, Constable Jones was forced to lock one man in the office area. However, this allowed the inmate's sister to pass him an axe through the window, which he used to chop around the door. He then removed the door from its frame and left. The axe marks are visible to this day. One lady, unhappy with having been locked up for drunkenness, placed a stone at the end of her stocking, and when next she passed the constable on the street, flung the device at his head.

Axe marks on the Tweed jail are reminders of an early breakout.

Once touted as North America's smallest lock-up, Tweed's jail is again a police facility.

The Depression saw many unemployed men passing through Tweed on one of its two railway lines, always searching for work. But rather than allowing them to sleep in local barns, an unpopular arrangement, the town council opened the cells, paying the jailer to house and feed them. While drunks and itinerants were the most common guests, the jail was briefly home to a crazed murderer from a more northern village named Cloyne, located just south of the present-day Bon Echo Park. After having joined a local religious cult known as the Hornerites,[17] he came to believe that his wife was the devil and was preparing to kill him with a snake. In a religious fit, he caved in her skull with a rock. After boasting of his deed, he was arrested and placed in the Tweed jailhouse to await the train, which would transfer him to the courthouse in Napanee.

When a new municipal hall was opened in 1950, with new cells located in it, the Tweed jail was closed. In 1965, it became a tourist information office, and posted the claim that here stood North America's smallest jail. That claim stood until the jails at Creemore, Rodney and Port Dalhousie all proved to be smaller. In 1995, its role changed once again when the OPP opened a community police station, replacing the three small cells with one large one. In this way Tweed's historic lock-up has returned to its roots.

Beside the jail stands the original town hall where the bars can still be seen in the tiny basement window of Tweed's first jail cell. Across the road, the Tweed Heritage Centre contains a museum and extensive archives that contain many early stories of the town's tiny jail. Tweed lies on Highway 37 about 35 kilometres north of Belleville. The jail can be found at the south end of the main street.

## UNIONVILLE

The one-time village of Unionville is a heritage time capsule. What began as a Pennsylvania-German mill village grew into a bustling railway town with an architectural mix of main street stores and houses.

When Toronto's urban sprawl began to creep towards Unionville in the 1960s, the planners of the day decided to widen the picturesque main street into four lanes to accommodate the rush of traffic. Concerned that this would destroy the ambience of the village, the very reason they lived there, the residents loudly protested. The planners listened and re-routed the four-lane road to bypass the village. Now, because it has been so well-preserved, Unionville's main street has become a popular day-trip destination from throughout the entire Greater Toronto Area. Here visitors can find an old hotel, a former wagon factory, a replica of the mill, and shops that once housed general stores, tailors, cobblers and blacksmiths, all of which have been converted to gift shops or cafes. To round off the historic integrity, even the original train station and adjacent feed mill have been saved.

This house in Unionville served briefly as the lock-up in this heritage village.

What is more difficult to spot, however, is the little house that served briefly as the jail. It lies at 145 Main Street, (this is not today's "main street" but rather a branch of the main street which follows the original surveyed road). Built in 1845 as a private dwelling, it was first owned by Neil McKinnon. In 1854, the owner of the sash and door mill bought it as a residence for his brother. The brother, George Eakin, was the council's treasurer and placed bars on the windows and installed secure doors to keep the treasury safe from theft. The building indeed does not resemble a jail, but rather looks like the board and batten cabin it originally was. The security provided at Eakin's house proved to be ideal for use as a temporary lock-up as well. With trains calling frequently on the Coboconk line, and with a busy hotel on the main street, the villagers had to endure their share of drunks and rowdies. The lock-up served as the ideal place for them to cool off overnight. Within a few years, however, a more permanent facility was built in nearby Markham. More recently, the original jail became a hairdresser's salon and then finally a private residence.

In 1907, the town was incorporated as a police village giving a board of trustees responsibility for fire protection, roads and policing. The first constable, Frank Frisby, was hired in 1915 and, among other things, enforced the snow-shovelling bylaw and the village's 15 mph speed limit.

Unionville's main street lies north of Highway 7 and west of Kennedy Road in what is now the expanded Town of Markham.

## WOODSLEE

The little Woodslee jail is not only far from home, it is far from being a jail. The settlement grew as a small railway town on the Michigan Central Railway in southwestern Ontario. With railway crews coming and going, along with transient workers and hotel rowdies, the little village decided to build a small brick jail.

In 1895, the four cell lock-up, which measured 6.5 metres by 9.5 metres, was opened for business. For a few years it was home to the usual assortment of drunks and vagrants. In 1899, a hotel keeper was fined for selling ginger to a minor, and likely spent some time in the jail. Miscreants would not only have to put up with one of four cramped cells, but also the lack of heating and plumbing. But its years as purely a jailhouse were short-lived. In 1900, it was used as a barber

*Above*, the Woodslee jail is now far from home in a heritage park; *below*, the interior of the Woodslee lock-up has been restored as a jail.

shop and later served as a polling station and a meeting hall for the Women's Institute. From 1982 to 1988 it housed a ceramics school, the last set of folks to use the jail. Having been declared unsafe, the jail was then scheduled for demolition.

In 1996, a movement to save the historic building raised $10,000. That meant, however, that it had to be disassembled and moved to its current home in the Southwest Ontario Heritage Village, located near the Town of Essex. Here, too, are log cabins, a church, a general store and a railway station, all moved from threatened locations to find a safe heritage haven. While the jail originally had four small cells, the restored version contains only two cells. Many of the furnishings inside relate to its days as the local lock-up, and include a pot-bellied stove and a magistrate's desk.

The Heritage Village, open only seasonally, is on Essex County Road 23 near the intersection with County Road 18 about 12 kilometres south of the Town of Essex.

## YORKVILLE

It may be stretching it a bit to think of the little brick antique shop in the heart of Toronto's trendy Yorkville as a jail. Yet, early in the history of this colourful little village, that is exactly the role this building performed.

Yorkville began to develop shortly after the government laid out Yonge Street from Lake Ontario to Lake Simcoe in 1794, and surveyed an east-west farm road known as Concession One (today's Bloor Street) As happened on many of Ontario's early roads, a toll booth was erected, this one at the intersection of the two primitive trails. Because travellers needed to stop anyway, taverns were commonly built near toll gates. To whet the whistles of those fuming over the tolls, the Red Lion and Wigwag taverns opened their doors on Yonge Street, a short distance north of the concession road. Later, in 1850, the water flow in Severn's Creek, just east of Yonge, attracted the attention of a pair of breweries. Workers began to arrive in the area and the small village of Yorkville was laid out on the west side of Yonge Street.

As the village grew, it became incorporated and added a tall brick town hall to its landscape. In 1867, John Daniels was hired as the village constable and built a small brick cottage on the southwest corner of what is today Yorkville and Bellair. Equipped with his sidearm (used mostly to shoot stray animals), Daniels would house drunks and rowdies in small wooden sheds which he built behind the house. In 1876, the town added a fire hall, located on the north side of Yorkville also east of Yonge.

Now part of Yorkville's upscale shopping district, this shop once housed the village jailer.

Then, in 1883, with Toronto expanding steadily towards the little country town, Yorkville's residents petitioned to have the city annex them. This would entitle them to the kinds of services that a city was able to provide—sidewalks, water and full-time policing. With his constabulatory services no longer needed, Daniels sold his little house to a watchmaker. Today the building has been modernized and enlarged to accommodate an antique store.

As for Yorkville's other key buildings, the town hall managed to survive into the 1940s, only to burn down. The two taverns were demolished. Yorkville has undergone several transformations over its lifetime—from country village to Toronto suburb, to hippy haven and now to upscale shopping district. And throughout it all, the little "jail" has managed somehow to persevere.

# 4

# THE BIG HOUSES

A new era in criminal punishment began with the conception of a penitentiary at Kingston. For centuries, punishments for crimes committed were usually exile or death. Incarceration was seldom used. But in the late 18th century, punishment and reform began to gain popularity, and the "penitentiary" was born. The first two experiments in North America were at Philadelphia where prisoners were kept constantly segregated, and at Auburn, New York, where they toiled communally during the day and were locked up at night.

In Canada, the penitentiaries were left for criminals convicted of the most serious crimes. While the county jails were used to hold prisoners awaiting their court date, or for shorter sentences, the "big houses" held felons who were likely to be there for a number of years. Unlike the county jails that were administered by the province, with the creation of the Dominion of Canada in 1867 the "pens" came under the jurisdiction of the federal government, today's Corrections Canada.

## KINGSTON "PEN"

If any community in Ontario goes hand in hand with the word jail, it is Kingston. From the construction of the "Pen" in 1835, the Kingston area has become home to several other penal institutions, including those at Bath, Millhaven, Joyceville and, across from the Pen itself, the Women's Pen.

With the growth of Upper Canada, the need for such a penitentiary became evident. Two locations were considered—Hamilton and Hatters Bay near the village of Portsmouth outside of Kingston. Because

The Kingston Penitentiary has welcomed its reluctant guests for more than 170 years.

of the ease of water transport, the presence of the military, and the fact that the two commissioners choosing the site were from Kingston, the hill overlooking Hatters Bay was selected. In 1833, work on the plans drawn up by architect William Coverdale[1] began. The design was similar to that in Auburn, and consisted of four wings of cells, five storeys high and radiating out from a central circular rotunda from which guards could watch the convicts.

In 1834, although the south wing was completed, it remained unoccupied, as the government had yet to allocate funds to actually run it. Finally, in 1835, the first six prisoners were escorted inside. There they gazed at their new home—five tiers of cells that measured less than a metre wide and only a little more than two metres deep. The iron bedsteads were connected to the wall by hinges so that they could be raised during the day. When lowered, they filled the entire width of the cubical.

The rules were as austere as the living conditions. No prisoner could speak to another prisoner, or even look at them. To do so meant physical punishment, usually lashings with a cat-o-nine-tails. Prisoners could be confined to a coffin-sized box and receive lashes for such infractions as wearing two pairs of underwear, or having too many handkerchiefs on them. Meals consisted of bread, which was usually soggy, served with tea and pork, which was usually mouldy.

The Toronto *Globe* of 1846 was especially outspoken about the overall conditions, noting in particular that lashings were inflicted at least 300 times a month: "Who can tell the amount of evil passions, of

revenge and of malice that must be engendered by such treatment."
Several other newspapers across the province re-iterated the outcry.
Finally, in 1848, the Brown Commission[2] was created to look into the
conditions at the prison and the harsh wardenship of Henry Smith. He
was found to be guilty not just of cruelty, but of mismanagement and
making false statements. Commission members were especially
appalled at the whipping of a 12-year-old boy for merely laughing.

Smith's son, hired by his father as kitchen steward, was found to have
shot arrows at prisoners, spat in their mouths and drenched them with
a fire hose after which he punished them for having wet clothes. Smith
was also found to have embezzled the prison and, in 1849, despite
efforts by a rising young politician named John A. Macdonald to dis-
credit the findings of the commission, he was fired. It was later learned
that Warden Henry Smith had been sending his employees to vote for
Macdonald at election time. During the time of the Brown Commission,
the prison population had risen from 55 in its first year to nearly 500.

Following Smith's dismissal, physical punishments were drastically
reduced, but a new torture device was introduced, known as the
"shower." Here, the convict was strapped down and his head placed
face down in a wooden bucket. Water was poured into the bucket
until it covered the victim's face, and then slowly drained, each time
inducing the feeling of drowning. Over the years the "shower" was
replaced with similar water techniques such as "tubbing" and "hos-
ing." Corporal punishment was not banned until 1972, as floggings
continued to be a routine part of prison punishment.

From such a formidable redoubt, escapes might seem impossible.
But they did occur. In 1875, two convicts named Blake and Smith
managed to flee after Smith had broken through the arch in his cell
and wiggled out. He then picked the lock on Blake's cell. Both then
crawled through a window where the bars had earlier been sawn.
Unseen by guards on what was an exceptionally stormy night, they
broke into the carpenter's shop to get ropes and ladders. Then,
clothed in suits intended for released prisoners, they slipped over the
wall and into the night. While Smith made good his flight, Blake was
later captured. The careless guards who had been asleep, were fired.

The most publicized breakout was that of the colourfully named
Red Ryan in 1923. After starting a fire in a stable by the wall, Ryan and
four other long-term convicts used the smoke as a screen to place a

The warden's house at the Kingston Pen is now home to a revealing prison museum.

ladder against the wall and quickly scrambled over. Once outside, they stole a car and raced north out of the city. The warden and his men hurried after them, but their car soon sputtered to a halt. The four escapees made good their flight. Abandoning their getaway car near the hamlet of Glenburnie, the fugitives forced food and shelter from a farmer. Ryan and one other fled as far as Minneapolis where they resumed their bank robbing ways until they were ambushed by police who had lured them to the local post office. Ryan was wounded and taken back to Kingston, while his companion escaped but on the following day was shot dead by the police. Flogged and sentenced to 15 years, Ryan managed to get paroled after serving just ten of them. Despite assurances that he had reformed from no less a figure than Prime Minister R.B. Bennett, Ryan resumed his life of crime and, less than a year later, while robbing a bank in Sarnia was killed by police.

Most visitors to Portsmouth will see only the penitentiary entrance situated on King Street. The main entrance is a Tuscan portico with flanking columns and wings topped by a pediment and cupola, all constructed of stone. What they won't see, (one would hope) are the cell blocks with their series of rounded windows stretching two storeys high. The original dome from the central rotunda has long since disappeared leaving the building with a flat topped appearance. This structure can be seen rising above the wall from across the bay at the village of Portsmouth itself. Several other additions have occurred over the years but are of limited architectural appeal.

But the pen itself is not the only legacy that the institution has left on the landscape. Across the road, built with prisoner labour in 1873, stands the sturdy stone home for the prison's governor. Today it houses the Penitentiary Museum where primitive instruments of torture used in the prisons of the day, such as the "shower" and the "box," make it seem more like a house of horrors. The warden continued to occupy the house until 1933 when it was converted to administration offices for the prison.

Several other prison-related buildings stand throughout the Portsmouth area. High on a hill overlooking the village is the Church of the Good Thief,[3] a massive stone building constructed using convict labour and finished in 1894. Behind the governor's residence is the Women's Penitentiary completed in 1933 but recently closed. The striking main building, referred to as the "gatehouse" is a three-storey stone structure topped with a prominent domed cupola.

Of three limestone buildings built to house prison service staff, only one survives at the corner of King Street and Sir John A. Macdonald Boulevard. Further north on the boulevard, where the other two staff

Kingston's Women's Pen has recently closed.

homes stood, is a structure that often puzzles first time visitors to the area. While the most frequent guess is that it was once the gallows, the tall stone tower was in fact the prison's water tower. The elaborate design of the arches and the stonework seem out of place on what was otherwise a strictly functional structure.

And a short distance north of the tower, a stone house on the west side of the boulevard is the former dwelling for what was the prison farm, most of which is now a parking lot.

The "Pen" faces the south side of King Street at the intersection of Sir John A. McDonald Boulevard.

## TORONTO'S DON JAIL

Although they may not know it, thousands have seen the inside of Toronto's notorious Don Jail. And they were not even criminals. Rather, they were moviegoers, for the abandoned portion of the old jail has been used as a location for many Hollywood movies, the most recent being the award-winning *Chicago*.

The "Don" was Toronto's fourth attempt at a jail. The first, which lasted from 1800 to 1824, was located at the corner of King Street and Leader Lane, and was little more than a squat, unpainted wooden building with a hipped roof, surrounded by a tall cedar stockade. As York, as Toronto was then called, grew, the old jail quickly proved to be inadequate, and a new one was built further west on King (which was then Toronto's main street). The two-storey red brick building was likewise surrounded by a sturdy wooden wall, which also enclosed the gallows. It was on these gallows in 1838 that rebel leaders Samuel Lount and Peter Matthews were hanged for their part in the ill-fated 1837 Upper Canada Rebellion. Close by, the courthouse was built in an identical style. Beside the courthouse were the community stocks in which a woman was once confined for disorderly conduct. After it was closed, the building served as one of Toronto's first lunatic asylums. It was later remodelled to become the York Chambers, with the original main entrance being filled in to become a window. It was eventually demolished in 1957.

Then, in 1840, a third jail was built on the ground of York's original legislative buildings at Front and Berkeley streets. This one was designed in a panopticon concept, a design in which the cell blocks radiated outward from the central guard tower in order to allow for

Elaborate architecture marks the entrance to the now closed section of Toronto's Don Jail.

easy surveillance. It remained in use until 1860 and was demolished in 1885 to be replaced by a Consumers Gas building.

Then, in 1857, William Thomas was chosen to design a grand new jail facility, one which would endure for more than a century. Originally, the jail was to be another panoptic plan, with four cell blocks radiating out from the central administration building, which would contain a semi-circular rotunda. The model for his creation was the Pentonville Prison in London, England. But by the time it was finished in 1860, after Thomas had died, it had been reduced to two wings of cell blocks, where the cells faced outward toward outside corridors, rather than inward to a large central corridor. At the time, the site was rural, on a hill top overlooking the pastoral valley of the Don River.

While the surrounding area has become part of the city, the old jail has remained unchanged. The central section rises like a Greek Temple four storeys high. Marking the entranceway is an oversized arched doorway, flanked by four "columns" that appear to be bound by ropes of stone. In the central cell block, the walkways look over a three-storey atrium where, in the early days, the cries of flogged inmates would echo so that all could hear. Iron brackets, decorated with gargoyles in the form of serpents, support the walkways. The cells are typically tiny, measuring just 1.3 metres by 2.5 metres. Originally, the jailer lived in the front portion of the building until a separate "governor's" house was built sometime in the 1890s.

Likely the most colourful episode in the history of the jail was the time involving the notorious Boyd Gang. Named for its leader, Edwin Alonso Boyd, the band embarked on a bank-robbing spree which started in 1949. Two years later they were captured and sent to the "Don" to await their trial. Despite the security, they promptly escaped

Floggings were a way of warning prisoners in the Don Jail not to transgress. *Courtesy of Toronto Public Library (TRL): T 17187.*

using smuggled files. Once more, following the shooting of a policeman, they were caught, jailed, and once again managed to file their way out. Following an extensive search, the gang was cornered in a barn in North York, and captured. The two members responsible for the death of the officer, Leonard Jackson and Ed Suchan, were hanged back-to-back on December 16, 1952, while Boyd served out his sentence in the penitentiary in Kingston. He later moved to western Canada where he adopted a new identity.

Over the years 70 hangings took place on the gallows of the Don Jail. The last was in 1962. It was also the last execution to take place in Canada.

In the 1960s, a portion of the old jail was demolished to make way for a new wing, and, in 1977, the old section was closed entirely, the only inhabitant now said to be the ghost of a former inmate. The Don Jail is located on the north side of Gerrard Street at the corner of Broadview. The house, which formerly housed the governor, has survived as well.

## TORONTO: ONTARIO'S CENTRAL PRISON

The faint remains of yet another, now largely forgotten Toronto prison
are those of the Central Prison. Built on Strachan Avenue in Toronto's
west end, it was one of a trio of provincial government prisons proposed in 1868. The two others were at Kingston and Stratford. Constructed by the inmates themselves between 1871 and 1873, it was
built to relieve the chronic overcrowding at the Don Jail.

The building was designed by the Department of Public Works
architect, Kivas Tully, the prolific government architect who was
responsible for many jail and courthouse designs across Ontario. The
centre block rose three storeys and featured a domed cupola on the
roof. Inside, a library and classroom provided night school for the 366
inmates. When not in class, prisoners were locked away in the two
wings that stretched to the east and west and contained four levels of
cell. Workshops were located at the rear of each wing and included a
woollen mill, a blacksmith shop, a furniture shop, a shoe shop, a
kitchen and a bakery. Products from the prison were sold usually in
other jails and prisons, but sometimes as far away as New York.

Despite the apparent range of distractions, life was decidedly
unpleasant for those sent to the Central Prison. The philosophy was that
inmates were sent here not for rehabilitation, but for punishment. There
were few if any sentence reductions, and corporal punishments were
freely handed out. The rule of silence was strictly enforced and infractions were met with whippings, solitary confinement or being "ironed"
to the wall. So common were the beatings that the prison was labelled
at the time as a "terror to evil-doers." By 1895 the government had come

An early view of Toronto's short-lived Central Prison, designed by Kivas Tully and
built by inmates.

Only the chapel has survived from the Central Prison in Toronto.

under pressure to call a commission of inquiry into the alleged abuses, much as the Brown Commission had done in revealing abuses at the Kingston Pen in 1848. However, unlike the unfortunate Warden Smith in Kingston, the warden and his staff were fully exonerated.

Despite its size and range of activities, the prison was closed after just forty years and taken over in 1915 by the military. Prisoners were relocated to a different form of confinement, for youth to the reformatory at Guelph, and, for the more hardened criminal, to the distant prison farm near the remote northern community of Burwash.

In 1920, some portions of the Central Prison were demolished, while other were portions incorporated into the adjacent Inglis Manufacturing Company. Today even that massive complex has been demolished to make way for a condominium development. The only remnant of the notorious Central Prison to survive is the chapel building. Protected now by an agreement between the owners of the land and the City of Toronto, the old red brick structure stands out in stark contrast to the modern buildings that huddle around it.

# Notes

## CHAPTER ONE—GOING TO GAOL

1  Diodorus Siculus (90-30 BC) was a Greek historian from Agyrium who wrote 40 books which he called the Library of History. In them he described the Roman prison at Alba Lucens, a settlement halfway between Rome and the Adriatic coast.

2  Sallust was a Roman historian and politician who lived between 86 and 34 BC. In his "Conspiracy of Cataline" he described life in the Roman era, including the conditions in the prison at the Roman Forum.

3  Before the creation of Upper Canada, most lock-ups were located in military garrisons, one of which was near Gananoque. It may have contained a lock-up facility.

4  With the influx of many United Empire Loyalists following the American Revolution, the old Province of Quebec was divided into Upper (later Ontario) and Lower (later Quebec) Canada in 1791. Lieutenant-Governor John Graves Simcoe was sent by Britain to be the administrator of Upper Canada.

5  In 1788, prior to the creation of Upper Canada, when the area now known as Ontario was part of the Province of Quebec, the first four administrative districts were created. The first counties began to appear in 1792 and by 1851 numbered more than two dozen. Prior to the recent spate of combining counties into regions, Ontario counted 42 counties and one provisional county (Haliburton). Northern Ontario remained divided into districts.

6  Police villages were a form of municipal structure created by the county within which they were found. With limited powers, police villages had no municipal council nor could they collect taxes. They consisted only of a Board of Police whose sole responsibility was to pass local bylaws, and maintain public order. Police villages no longer exist.

7  The beginnings of the Ontario Provincial Police date back to 1875 with James Wilson Murray heading a staff of government detectives in the office of the Attorney General. In 1909, an order-in-council created an Ontario Provincial Police force consisting originally of six inspectors and 38 constables. The OPP today maintains a museum in its Orillia headquarters. Here the visitor can view uniforms, restraining devices, motorcycles and a restored 1941 Chevrolet Master Deluxe Coupe patrol car.

8  Before women had a separate facility, the first three female inmates in Kingston were housed in the prison hospital. In 1839, they were placed in their own wing in the main penitentiary. In 1934, they moved into a prison of their own on the north side of King Street opposite the now all-male pen. The women's pen closed July 6, 2000.

9  Quote from the Board of Inspectors is from the Ontario Department of Provincial Secretary, "Report on Common Gaols, Prisons and Asylums," 1860. Herinafter called "Report on Common Gaols, Prisons and Asylums."

10  "Report on Common Gaols, Prisons and Asylums," 1881.

11  Ibid, 1860.

12  The oldest of Ontario's county jails were the worst, many of them dating back to before there were even any counties. Cells were tiny, dark and poorly ventilated while the sanitary facilities were badly outdated. Among the dingiest were the Middlesex County jail in London, the Carleton County jail in Ottawa and the Waterloo County jail in Kitchener.

## CHAPTER TWO—THE COUNTY GAOLS

1 Thomas Young, born in England circa 1805, was known as an artist, teacher, architect, politician, civil engineer and surveyor. By 1834 he was settled in Toronto and was the drawing master at Upper Canada College. He remained active as an artist, but soon acquired greater recognition as an architect. His first architectural work in Toronto seems to have been a house and outbuildings for Robert Baldwin Sullivan, completed in 1836. He secured major commissions from three new administration districts (Wellington, Huron and Simcoe) and was the architect for the Wellington District jail (1839–40) and the courthouse at Guelph (1842-44), the Huron District jail at Goderich (1839-42) at Goderich and the Simcoe District jail (1840-41) at Barrie.

  For a brief period he served as a councilman for St. Andrews Ward (1839-40) in Toronto and employed part-time by the city as architect, engineer and surveyor. He died suddenly in 1860 and was buried in St. James Cemetery. For more information, see the Dictionary of Canadian Biography Online at www.biographi.ca, accessed July 4, 2006.

2 The reference to "mosque of Omar" is from Andrew F. Hunter, *A History of Simcoe County: Part I, Its Public Affairs* (originally published in 1909, reproduced by the History Committee of Simcoe County in 1948) 249.

3 "Report on Common Gaols, Prisons and Asylums," 1876.

4 Huey Newton's quote is from a photocopy of a newspaper in a file on the Peel County Jail, Peel Museum Complex, Brampton, Ontario.

5 Ibid.

6 Tong wars were often waged among groups of Chinese immigrants to North American cities. Many of these rival gangs operated gambling parlours and opium dens, yet often consisted of some of the community's leading business owners. The term "tong" refers to a Chinese guild, association or secret society.

7 Taken from a photocopy of a newspaper (not dated). Local History File, Brantford Public Library.

8 Today, Johnstown is a quiet rural suburb of Brockville. An historic plaque and prisoner's stocks mark the location of the courthouse and jail.

9   William Buell was born in Connecticut but sided with the British during the American Revolution and went to Montreal to join the Loyalist forces. At the end of hostilities he was entitled to five hundred acres as an officer and one hundred acres for his wife and child. He opened a general store on his land (Elizabethtown), followed by a sawmill and gristmill. He later was appointed a justice of the peace and represented Leeds in parliament. He died of cholera in 1832. For more information, see Russ Disotell, *Brockville: The River City* (Toronto: Natural Heritage Books, 1997).

10  John George Howard was born in Hertfordshire, England, in 1803, and in 1824 was articled to a London architect for three years. His birth name was John Corby. He changed his surname to Howard upon arrival in York, Canada, in 1832. For more details, see the Dictionary of Canadian Biography Online at www.biographi.ca.

Like Thomas Young, he taught drawing at Upper Canada College, remaining there until about 1856. His architectural drawings came to the attention of prominent people and Howard soon began receiving commissions. In the 1830s and 1840s, he was one of the busiest architects in Upper Canada, designing many houses, shops and offices and about a dozen churches, generally for the Church of England.

His major work was the Provincial Lunatic Asylum in Toronto (1845-49), an immense building in the local white brick that had been introduced into practice. The building was demolished by the provincial government in 1976. Among the number of public buildings designed by John Howard are Toronto's third jail (1840) and the Brockville courthouse and jail (1841–43). In 1843, he succeeded Thomas Young as city surveyor.

By 1855, he was generally retired and spending much time working on the extensive grounds of Colborne Lodge. He had bought the land in 1836 for a sheep farm. In 1873, in return for a yearly pension of $1,200, John Howard deeded 120 acres of his property to the city as a public park to be called High Park. The remaining 45 acres and his home (Colborne Lodge) became city property upon his death. The City of Toronto added 241 acres to High Park. Today, his home, a significant sample of his Regency cottage design is a museum that features a number of his watercolour paintings.

John Howard died at Colborne Lodge, Toronto, in 1890.

11  Little could be found on Henry Horsey other than he practised architecture in both Kingston and Ottawa at various times. He was the architect for the Perth County jail.

12  The Townsend Gang, led by William Townsend, included George King, William Bryson and John Blowes, operated on both sides of the border and were finally broken up by Ontario Crown Attorney Richard Martin. Apparently, they had little luck in obtaining large sums of money from their heists. Their efforts to rob a man named John Nelles, a merchant from Cayuga, Ontario, resulted in his being murdered in his home on October 18, 1854. While King and Blowes were both teenagers when executed, the actual leader, Townsend, was never captured.

13  Olive Sternaman was found guilty and was sentenced to hang. At the last moment she was pardoned. See Cheryl MacDonald, *Who Killed George?: The Ordeal of Olive Sternaman* (Toronto: Natural Heritage Books, 1994).

14  Chatham's W.I.S.H. Centre (Woodstock Institute Sertona Help Centre) houses much material on the Black Heritage of Chatham-Kent. Operated by the Black History Society it contains many accounts and artifacts representing the struggles of the area's fugitive slaves. Gwen Johnson of Chatham, a major force in the setting up of the W.I.S.H. Centre, continues to work with the centre.

15  The quote is from an anonymous commentator, as quoted in a photocopy of a newspaper (not dated) in the Local History File, Chatham Public Library.

16  William Thomas, architect, water-colourist and engineer was born in Suffolk, England, in 1799. His architectural work in England encompasses an exceptional range of structures from houses, shops and churches to a conservatory, a public bath complex and iron and stone bridges.

In the spring of 1843, William Thomas emigrated to Toronto with his wife and eight children. Among the many churches he designed in Toronto was St. Michael's Cathedral (1845-48), constructed of the then-fashionable white brick. He was kept busy designing a succession of significant public buildings, including the Talbot District Jail in Simcoe (1847–48), the Kent County Courthouse, Chatham (1848–49), the St. Lawrence Hall, Arcade and Market building, Toronto (1849-51), the Don Jail, Toronto

(1859–64), the town hall and market, Guelph (1856-57) and the town hall and market, Stratford, (1857).

In 1857 two of his sons, William Tutin and Cyrus Pole, whom he had trained, became part of his firm, now known as William Thomas and Sons. William Thomas died in 1860 and was buried in the family's plot at St. James Cemetery. For more information, see the Dictionary of Canadian Biography Online at www.biographi.ca, accessed July 4, 2006.

17  "Report on Common Gaols, Prisons and Asylums," 1866.

18  Ibid, 1872.

19  The magnificent Victoria Hall was designed by Ontario's provincial architect, Kivas Tully, to rival Toronto's St. Lawrence Hall. It was opened by the Prince of Wales in 1860 and today has been restored to house an art gallery, and concert hall. It contains offices of the mayor and council chambers and a fully functioning courtroom modelled on London's Old Bailey.

Kivas Tully, architect, civil engineer and civil servant was born in Garryvacum in Ireland. In 1834, he emigrated to Toronto where his elder brother was in the office of John Howard, gaining experience towards his license as a land surveyor.

In 1851, he won commissions for the Welland County Court-House at Welland and in 1852 for Cobourg's town hall, Victoria Hall, which remains as Tully best-known work. As well as designing numerous buildings and churches, he was appointed engineer for the Toronto Harbour Trust, and was involved in planning an esplanade to give access to Toronto's wharves after the railways, then under construction were completed.

Following Confederation, he joined the new Ontario Department of Public Works and was appointed the department's architect, engineer and chief officer. He saw to the completion of the parliament buildings (Queen's Park) 1893, and courthouses at North Bay (1888) and Gore Bay (1889), among other places. Kivas Tully died in 1905. For more information, see the Dictionary of Canadian Biography Online at www.biographi.ca, accessed on July 4, 2006.

20  New Johnstown was named in honour of Sir John Johnson, who led a group of disbanded soldiers and Loyalist refugees to freedom in Upper Canada following the American Revolution. He supervised the resettling of the Loyalists along the upper St. Lawrence in 1784.

21  For more information on the Canada Company and the Huron Tract, see Robert C. Lee, *The Canada Company and the Huron Tract, 1826-1853: Personalities, Profits and Politics* (Toronto: Natural Heritage Books, 2004).

22  Two of the more comprehensive books on the saga of the feud are the *Donnelly Family Album* by Ray Fazakas (Toronto: Firefly Books, 1995) and *Night Justice: The True Story of the Black Donnellys* by Peter Edwards (Toronto: Key Porter Books, 2004).

23  The Truscott case had come up for review in 2005 and 2006 and is still not resolved. For a brief overview, see "Steven Truscott: A Struggle for Justice" in George Sherwood's *Legends In Their Time: Young Heroes and Victims of Canada* (Toronto: Natural Heritage Books, 2006).

24  The last public hanging was in Ottawa, according to Corrections Canada. Public hangings fell out of the public taste and considered too ghoulish for most people, especially when the hangings occasionally involved accidental dismemberment. Prime Minister John A. Macdonald amended the Criminal Code in 1868 to limit capital offences to murder, treason and rape. It was likely amended at this time to prohibit public hangings, although the public could continue to view executions but only by invitation. The last of these occurred at Montreal's Bordeaux jail in 1935, when the hanging did in fact decapitate the convicted felon. Some argue that the last "public" hanging was that of Louis Riel in 1885 and his co-defendants. While there was a large audience, the executions occurred within the RCMP compound and the viewers were there by invitation.

25  One of the rare examples of a poorhouse is the Wellington County House of Industry. Today, it houses the Wellington County Museum and Archives.

26  Quote taken from "Report of Common Gaols, Prisons and Asylums," Huron County Gaols, 1875.

27  The concept of a "Canadian plan" for jails is taken from an interview with Nicole Weppler, Curator of the Gore Bay Museum.

28  William Mahoney was the leading architect in Guelph during the first half of the 20th century. He made his reputation designing plain, functional buildings. Information taken from Hilary Stead, *Guelph: A People's Heritage 1827–2002*, on www.electricscotland.com, accessed July 5, 2006.

29 The Waterloo County Gaol is the oldest county building in the Waterloo Region. After housing prisoners continuously for 125 years, it was closed by the Ministry of Correctional Services in 1978. The Governor's house had been added in 1878. Although considered for demolition, a group of dedicated people saved the historic structures. The redevelopment and adaptive reuse was approved as a Millennium Project in 1999. The exteriors are designated under the Ontario Heritage Act. Today, the refurbished buildings house two courtrooms with the Governor's House providing office space and public meeting space. Historical and archaeological displays are in the lobby. Taken from www.region.waterloo.on.ca, accessed on July 5, 2006.

30 The quote is attributed to a "local person" in a photocopy of a newspaper (not dated) in the Local History File, Waterloo Region Public Library.

31 "Grand Jury Report on the Waterloo County Jail," Office of the Ontario Attorney General, 1977.

32 The Ventin Group Ltd., Architects was founded in 1972 in Simcoe, Ontario. In 1975, Carlos Ventin was hired to demolish the old 19th century courthouse and jail. Going against popular thinking of the time, he convinced the local politicians to convert it to a municipal office and library. The award-winning project was on the leading edge of heritage preservation in Canada and caught the attention of many municipalities. The firm has completed more than 50 similar projects and has received many awards. Taken from www.ventin-group.com, accessed on July 5, 2006.

33 "Report on Common Gaols, Prisons and Asylums," 1875, 1876.

34 Following the suppression of the Rebellion of 1837 in York, a number of rebels escaped to the United States. Over the next year, some of these Canadian exiles, along with American supporters, conducted a series of cross-border raids. In December of 1938, a group crossed from Windsor to Detroit in the so-called "Windsor Raid." Forty-three of them were captured; some were arbitrarily shot. As a result of their trial, held that December, six men were hanged: Daniel D. Bedford, Albert Clark, Cornelius Cunningham, Joshua G. Doan, Hiram B. Lynn and Amos Perly. See Edwin Guillett, *Lives and Times of the Patriots* (Toronto: University of Toronto Press, 1968; originally published in 1938 by Thomas Nelson). The list of names of those executed is in Appendix O, 286-89.

35  The quote is taken from a display in the museum section of the county jail.

36  Taken from the verbal tour commentary, Donnelly Family Homestead Site.

37  "Report on Common Gaols, Prisons and Asylums," Report on Russell County Gaol, 1874.

38  Ibid.

39  Ibid, Report on Halton County Gaol, 1876.

40  Bytown, named after Colonel John By of the Royal Engineers, whose men built the Rideau Canal, was renamed Ottawa after the river in 1854. Ottawa was chosen as the capital in 1857.

41  *Ottawa Citizen*, October 18, 1862.

42  Thomas D'Arcy McGee was an Irishman who published the *New Era* newspaper in Montreal in which he called for the federation of Britain's North American colonies. Along with John A. Macdonald and George-Étienne Cartier, he was considered one of the main Fathers of Confederation. He was assassinated in 1868 for the views he expressed on the violence of the Fenians.

43  William Wye Smith, *Gazetteer for the County of Grey*, 1865-6 (Toronto: 1866.)

44  This is the version depicted in the official history of the OPP. Local accounts claim that three robbers were involved and that Burowski alone was in the stolen vehicle. For more information, see Adrian Hayes, *Parry Sound: Gateway to Northern Ontario* (Toronto: Natural Heritage Books, 2005) 146-157, and Adrian Hayes, *Murder and Mayhem at Waubamik* (Markham, ON: Stewart Publishing, 2002).

45  From a photocopy of the *Parry Sound North Star*, 1903, in the Local History File, Parry Sound Public Library.

46  In the 19th century, indentureship was a form of unpaid labour whereby the worker could gain citizenship in exchange for work. It was illegal to flee from the workplace as this was a breach of contract. This is found in the 1862 report of the Sheriff of Bathurst District.

47  From a photocopy of the *Perth Courier* (not dated), in the Local History File, Perth Public Library.

48  Ibid.

49  "Report of the Inspector of Jails," Upper Canada, 1842.

50 "Report on Common Gaols, Prisons and Asylums," Report on Norfolk County Gaol, 1863.

51 William Dunlop was born in Scotland in 1792 and trained as a doctor in Glasgow and London. He was in Canada in 1813 and treated the wounded from the War of 1812-14. John Galt (also Scottish) was the first commissioner of the Canada Company. A friendship developed between the two men. In 1834, Dunlop was appointed the Canada Company's Warden of the Forests and was instrumental in the settlement of the Huron Tract. He died in 1848 and was buried at Goderich. See Robert C. Lee, *The Canada Company and the Huron Tract, 1826–1853: Personalities, Profits and Politics* (Toronto: Natural Heritage Books, 2004). For more details, see Gary Draper and Roger Hall, "Dunlop, William" in *Dictionary of Canadian Biography*, Volume vii (Toronto: University of Toronto Press, 1988) 260-64.

52 "Report of [County of Perth] Reeves' Committee on Plans and Specifications" [for the proposed new gaol], 1851.

53 Ibid.

54 "Report on Common Gaols, Prisons and Asylums," Report on Perth County Gaol, 1868.

55 Ibid, 1871.

56 *Illustrated Historical Atlas of County of Perth,* H. Belden and Co., republished by Mika Publishing of Belleville, 1972, originally published in 1879.

57 "Report on Common Gaols, Prisons and Asylums," Report on Perth County Gaol, 1884.

58 It is not known what happened afterwards to either the hangman or the doctor.

59 "Report on Common Gaols, Prisons and Asylums," Report on Welland County Gaols, 1884.

60 Ibid.

61 Ibid.

62 Fenians were a 19th century nationalist organization founded among the Irish in the U.S. Their members encouraged revolutionary activities aimed at overthrowing the British government in Ireland. Part of their activities included raids into Canada from the U.S.

63 *Woodstock Daily Sentinel-Review,* November 2, 1907.

64 Ibid.

## CHAPTER THREE—THE LOCAL LOCKUPS

1  *Beaverton Express*, 1896, from a photocopy in the Local History File, Beaverton Public Library.

2  Ibid.

3  Ibid.

4  Cornish miners were actively recruited by Canadian mining companies because of their experience working in difficult mining conditions. Many were unemployed following the tin mine closures in Cornwall, England.

5  For background information on the colonial government's negotiations of the surrender of the Saugeen Peninsula, see Mel Atkey, *When We Both Got to Heaven: James Atkey Among the Anishnabek at Colpoy's Bay* (Toronto: Natural Heritage Books, 2002) 75-134.

6  *Creemore Star* (not dated), from a photocopy displayed in the Creemore Gaol Museum.

7  Conversation with Chris Raible of Creemore on July 11, 2006. He believes this to be true, but has yet to find any documentation to verify this description.

8  Quote is from a newspaper as quoted in Andrew F. Hunter's *A History of Simcoe County*.

9  Ibid.

10  *Madoc Mercury*, May 10, 1869, microfiche in the Madoc Public Library.

11  The first Welland Canal was the dream of William Hamilton Merrit. The canal was badly needed to eliminate the tedious portage around the falls of Niagara. The first canal opened in 1829 with 40 locks between Lakes Ontario and Erie. Today's canal, the fourth one to be built, needs only seven locks.

12  This is a term that Manitoulin Islanders call themselves as many of their ancestral settlers supplemented their meagre diet by eating the local hawberries.

13  From Elinor Barr, *Silver Islet: Striking It Rich in Lake Superior* (Toronto: Natural Heritage Books, 1988) 125.

14  Beryl Scott, "Silver Islet Landing," in *Canadian Geographic Journal*, Vol. 52, #3, March 1956, 127.

15  Lorne Saxberg, CBC broadcaster, died suddenly on May 6, 2006, following an accident while snorkelling in Thailand.

16 From the Local History File, Tweed Heritage Centre, Tweed, Ontario.

17 The Hornerites, also known as the Holiness Movement, were an offshoot of the Methodist Church. The movement began in the 1830s in New York City. Their religion called for personal regeneration through spiritual experiences, which often took the form of speaking in tongues and rolling on the floor in apparent convulsions. (This behaviour earned them the nickname "holy rollers.") The Census of Canada in 1901 counted 2,775 members of the Holiness Movement. A small congregation exists today in the area of Ompah and Mazinaw, northeast of Tweed, Ontario.

## CHAPTER FOUR—THE BIG HOUSES

1 William Coverdale, the City of Kingston architect from 1846-65, designed many of the city's grander buildings including the Rosemount Inn. He believed that society could be shaped by architecture.

2 In 1848, the Legislative Assembly of Canada West (later Ontario) established a Commission of Enquiry to examine conditions in the then provincial penitentiary at Kingston. A report was completed in 1849 listing a litany of abuses including excessive floggings for breaking silence rules and floggings imposed on inmates as young as 12 years of age. While the warden was replaced, many of the abuses continued.

3 The Church of the Good Thief was completed in 1894 at a cost of $14,297. Prisoners from the nearby penitentiary were paid 25 cents a day to quarry the rocks from a local quarry. The name of the church had nothing to do with the source of its labour, but rather it was named for St. Dismas, the biblical thief who perished on a cross beside Jesus.

# Bibliography

Assiginack Museum Board, *A Time to Remember: A History of the Municipality of Assiginack* (Manitowaning, ON: The Society, 1996).

Auchinleck, J., April Braley, Liza Mallyon, Tammy Poot, "The Mad, the Bad and the Wretched, the Cobourg County Jail 1865–1875," in *Canadian Studies Research Project, 475*, Trent University, 1992.

Barber, Marla Adamson, *The Formative Years of Bruce Mines: A Social History* (K.E. Jeglum, ed.) (Dollup and Marx, Attic Press, 1991).

Brookes, Geoffrey, "A Short History of Rodney Village" not dated.

Byers, Mary, and Margaret McBurney, "Prison Reform...the Oxford County Jail," in *Ontario Living*, October 1987, 44g–44h.

Canaran, Hement R., "Recycling old jails for new community uses," in *Municipal World*, February 1989.

Curtis D., et al, *Kingston Penitentiary: The First Hundred and Fifty Years, 1835–1985* (Ottawa: Correctional Service of Canada, 1985).

Eadie, James A., *Behind the Limestone Walls: The Old County Gaol in Napanee* (Napanee, ON: Lennox and Addington County Museum, 1989).

Gaols of Ontario, www.canadiancorrections.com, accessed in 2003. The site no longer exists.

*Globe and Mail*, "The Way It Was: Woodstock Gaol," February 1, 1977.

"Guide to Doors Open London, 2003," promotional blurb for Doors Open London.

Hart, Hastings H., *Plans for City Police Jails and Village Lockups* (New York: Russell Sage Foundation, 1932).

Hayes, Adrian, *Murder and Mayhem at Waubamik: The Shooting of Thomas Jackson* (Markham, ON: Stewart Publishing, 2002).

Hennessy, Peter H., *Canada's Big House: The Dark History of the Kingston Penitentiary* (Toronto: Dundurn Press, 1999).

*H-Block and Court House Hill Walking Tour*, booklet published by Heritage Barrie, not dated.

*Heritage Assessment of the Court House, L'Orignal Ontario* (Heritage Research Associates Inc., 2001).

Higley, Dahn D., *The History of the Ontario Provincial Police Force* (Toronto: Ontario Provincial Police, 1984).

Hudson, Brenda M., *Fabric of a Dream: A Settlement Story of Madoc and Elzevir Township* (Belleville, ON: Mika Publishing, 1979).

Hunter, Andrew F., *A History of Simcoe County, 1863–1940* (Barrie, ON: Historical Committee of Simcoe County, 1948).

"Huron Historic Gaol: Interesting Facts," pamphlet published by the Huron County Museum, not dated.

Johnston, Norman B., *The Human Cage: A Brief History of Prison Architecture* (New York: Published for the American Foundation, Institute of Corrections, by Walker, 1973).

Kidd, Martha Ann, "Historical Sketches of Peterborough: Part IX, The County Courthouse and Jail," in *Prime Time*, October 1995.

"The District of Johnstown Court House and Gaol: Designation Report," produced by LACAC of Brockville, June 1, 1979.

*Designated Buildings and Structures of Architectural and Historic Interest in the City of Guelph, 1977–1994*, booklet published by LACAC of the City of Guelph, 1995.

Oliver, Peter, *Terror to Evil-Doers: Prisons and Punishments in Nineteenth-Century Ontario* (Toronto: Published for the Osgoode Society for Canadian Legal History by University of Toronto Press, 1998).

"Parry Sound Jail" (Parry Sound Public Library, 1999).

"District Court House stands as link with Parry Sound's Past," *Parry Sound North Star*, September 1983.

Strachan Stephanie, "Perth Jail: Recognizing the rich history of a landmark" in *Perth Courier*, October 10, 1994.

"The Day the Gallows Saw its Last Customer" in *Peterborough This Week*, September 17, 1997.

"Small Gaols of Ontario, Ontario's Village Constabulary Gaol Trail," www.canadiancorrections.com, accessed in 2003. The site no longer exists.

Talbot, C.K., *Justice in Early Ontario: Part III, District Jails* (Ottawa: Crimcare, 1983).

"Murder Suspect Held in Tweed Jail," in *Tweed News,* July 1903.

"Some Interesting Reminiscences of Life in the Oxford County Jail," in *Woodstock Sentinel-Review*, November 1907.

# Index

# About the Author

Ron Brown is a geographer and travel writer who has explored Ontario's many back roads and remote regions in search of the unusual. To encourage today's generation to celebrate their heritage, he has written best-selling books on ghost towns, back roads and vestiges of a vanishing railway era. His titles have included *Ghost Towns of Ontario, Back Roads of Ontario,* and *The Last Stop: Ontario Heritage Railway Stations.* He has also written of Ontario's forgotten castles, its unusual main streets, and now presents a look inside Ontario's heritage "gaols." Drawn from his many titles, Ron Brown offers lectures on, and leads bus tours to those hidden treasures that may lie right in your own backyard.

Ron Brown has been a member of the Writer's Union of Canada since 1981 and has served as its treasurer and chair.